Magic Pencil

MAGIC PENCIL

Children's Book Illustration Today

Selected by Quentin Blake

The British Council / The British Library

Contents

Magic Pencil
A British Council Exhibition
Organised and toured by Visual Arts

Commissioning Editor: Andrea Rose
Selected by Quentin Blake
Organised by Diana Eccles and Louise Wright

This book is co-published by The British Council
and The British Library to accompany the
exhibition *Magic Pencil*, shown in Britain at:
Laing Art Gallery, Newcastle upon Tyne
9 May – 15 September 2002
The British Library, London
1 November 2002 – 31 March 2003

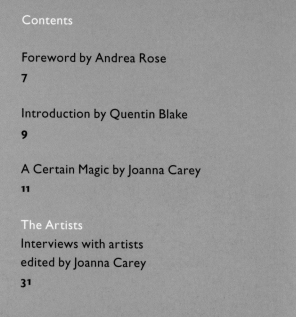

Angela Barrett
32

Patrick Benson
38

Foreword

'Why on earth show the original drawings?' asked one of the illustrators when the subject of an exhibition about the art of children's book illustration first came up. 'It's much simpler to see them in a book than to have them hanging round the walls.'

The answer is that, seeing the originals, as opposed to the printed books, is rather like being in a room with someone as distinct from having their photograph in front of you. You become aware of the subtleties and observations that go into the making of each page, and of the character that lies behind the images – the touch of John Burningham's pencil, for example, as he draws Aldo, the companion to a lonely child, or the astonishing focus of Stephen Biesty's cross-section drawings, so detailed they feel like virtual reality. Elsewhere in this book, Raymond Briggs talks about the Victorian illustrators whose work is 'so full of life before being transferred to the woodblock and engraved by people like the Dalziel Brothers'. Over a hundred years later, and despite the improvements in printing and reproduction, the gap between the sheet that leaves the studio and the published book is still pretty wide (and how often are those books only ever seen in the semi-dark, at bedtime?)

And seeing the originals reinforces the importance of these works. Children's books are where it all begins, so to speak, where first impressions of the world outside are formed. Even for children fed on video and TV a book concentrates and distils an image: it can be hand-held, slowed-down, pored over and re-examined in ways that no new technology replaces. Illustration needs no translation, but seeing it on a different scale, often without text, in sharper colour, and hanging on walls, is to see it in a new light. Britain has a long tradition of innovative book design and illustration, and the works of earlier generations of illustrators are known and loved worldwide. (For many, the illustrations to *Alice in Wonderland*, *Peter Rabbit* and *Winnie the Pooh* were their first introduction to British culture, and even perhaps its defining moment.) *Magic Pencil* shows how today's illustrators reflect contemporary concerns with equal force and originality; and how their work incontestably establishes this as a second golden age of British illustration.

We are extremely grateful to Quentin Blake, the first Children's Laureate, for having undertaken the selection for *Magic Pencil*. Blake's illustrations to *The Twits* and other works by Roald Dahl have become indelibly associated with Dahl's gleefully disgusting rhymes and tales, just as all great artists make the text they are illustrating unimaginable without their drawings. The rules for selection were fairly strict: artists had to be living, to be British (although that includes illustrators not born in the UK), and each was to be shown in some depth, meaning that their numbers would inevitably be limited. Some of his choices are so familiar as to be almost household names in Britain – Blake himself, Raymond Briggs, John Burningham, Tony Ross and Michael Foreman. Others represent new and varied ways of approaching book illustration, such as the use of integrated TV and photographic collages by Lauren Child, and the innovative layouts of Sara Fanelli using experimental type, hand-lettering and old papers collaged on to the artwork. Others such as Posy Simmonds

and Angela Barrett are not always associated with children's books: Posy
Simmonds' comic strips are well known to newspaper readers in Britain; and
Angela Barrett's black and white illustrations to *Candide* are, well, grown-up
and sexy. So, hardly a prescriptive choice about who and what a child might be.

The artists themselves have been unfailingly generous, and we would like
to thank them for their agreement to lend work for a considerable length of time,
to being interviewed, photographed and generally disturbed. We would also like to
thank Joanna Carey, formerly Children's Book Editor of *The Guardian*, for her lively
essay on children's book illustration past and present, which also encompasses
many contemporary illustrators whom we were unable to include in the exhibition.
And thanks too to Elizabeth Hammill, whose initiative in setting up the Centre for
the Children's Book in Newcastle upon Tyne has encouraged a renewed interest in
children's books, which in turn has made it possible to launch this exhibition and the
accompanying book at the Laing Art Gallery, Newcastle. Julie Milne and Samantha Hill
at the Laing Art Gallery and Alan Sterenberg and Heather Norman-Soderlind at
The British Library, London, have been invaluable partners in presenting this exhibition,
which has been organised in London with great dedication by my colleagues
Diana Eccles and Louise Wright. I should also like to extend my thanks to the many
other individuals who have contributed both to the exhibition and book, whose
names appear separately on the last page.

Andrea Rose
Director of Visual Arts
The British Council

Quentin Blake

Introduction

This book has been published to coincide with the British Council exhibition of the same name. If one can't expect always to find a show of original book illustrations such as this ready to hand, one can at least say that such a thing is not as rare as it once was; and that no doubt reflects an increased awareness of the art of illustration. To what extent is hard to quantify, and I can bring to the discussion only the tiniest anecdotal evidence – to the effect that when I was a child, though fascinated by drawings, I didn't have the concept of 'an illustrator', and that nowadays children write to me explaining that it is something they want to be when they grow up, and do I have any tips about how to arrange it?

Those who eventually achieve their ambition will come to experience, with those whose work appears in *Magic Pencil*, an assorted set of advantages and disadvantages. They may make a living (perhaps even a good one), but it is far from guaranteed; they may become popular – and it is fortifying to be brought copies of your books to sign and gratifying at the same time not to be recognised in the street. (Curious, too, at public signings to discover that people have been buying your books for years and sometimes even keeping them. It's quite possible, alone at your desk, to believe that the ensuing productions are taken by publishers and booksellers and buried quietly somewhere out of the way).

They may sense, too, if they illustrate books for children, that because the word 'children' is included in the description of the activity, it is in some way juvenile. In fact, many such illustrators have come from other areas – painting, graphic journalism, satire –and go on working for adult audiences in their own individual styles. Joanna Carey talks about this in her essay elsewhere in this book, where, by way of demonstration, you will also find work specifically for adults from more than one artist.

An artist who is setting out to illustrate a book for children will be, depending on temperament and talent, moved by personal impulses – by a vivid access to memories of childhood, or by parental affection, or by some hotline to youthful sentiments and reactions; or perhaps by an urge, not necessarily related to children, to draw toucans, polar bears, or intergalactic space cruisers. Whatever venture the illustrator may be embarked on, the answer to the question 'what is the illustrator thinking about?' is – a number of things at the same time. It's a complex twist of strands which may include: an imaginative response to the characters and activities in the story; the quality and convincingness of the drawing; what the role of colour is going to be and how it is going to be incorporated; how each page is going to be composed within itself and arranged in the sequence of pages that make up the book; which moments in the narrative are suitable for illustration, and (if the text is by another writer) whether modifications in style and atmosphere of the drawing are called for. And, of course, on another level, how the work on the book in hand is to fit into a timetable with other commissions to bring it satisfactorily to a conclusion before the publisher's deadline. So, childishly simple, really.

Illustrators have also sometimes experienced the disadvantage of what they do being called 'illustration' and the implied diminishing contrast between art that is 'commercial' and art that is 'fine'. The history of that development is well beyond me to rehearse, even if this were the place to do it, but it no doubt begins in those attempts in the Renaissance to establish painting as a high-level intellectual activity in which you didn't have to get your hands dirty, later reinforced by the Romantic notion of genius – something so attractive to artists and those who deal in their uncommercial works that it hovers comprehensively in the background even today. Having said that, I should emphasise that I do not mean to overstate illustration's achievements or possibilities; it is interesting to note, however, that this is art which, on its own scale, shares characteristics with earlier kinds of Western painting. An illustrator understands, as I have already suggested, about clients (although they are no longer religious or aristocratic ones), about storytelling in pictures, about so much work for so much money, about meeting (or failing to meet) the deadline; and knows that the image a curator refers to as an Old Master drawing is often something an illustrator recognises as a 'rough'.

What *Magic Pencil* as book and exhibition proposes is that, like works of former times, these originals repay inspection in their own right; and that contemplating them brings its own pleasures as well as enlarging our sense of how illustration works.

To select such an exhibition is enjoyable but not easy. This is a rich and crowded sea, and there is enormous diversity – imagine a shoal in which every fish is different. We have tried to reflect that diversity in the age and gender of the participants, and in the way they handle their materials and the way they respond to life. Impossible, in a travelling exhibition, to include more than a dozen or so artists if there is to be enough of the work of each to give the spectator a true sense of the individual, so that the painful part of the selection was the hard necessity to leave out many artists we admire, many artists whom the informed visitor might reasonably expect to encounter. Fortunately this book is not subject to quite such strict restraints and Joanna Carey's survey is able to outline a broader sense of British children's book illustration past and present: where we come from, where we are now, the range of artists at work in this field. Even so, we are conscious of many artists we have failed to mention. But this is an anthology, not an encyclopaedia.

Is it possible to discern amidst the diversity an approach, a flavour, a vision distinctive to these misty off-shore islands? Perhaps as this show travels there will be different and more distinct perceptions than we are able to achieve in looking at ourselves. We may hope, at least, that however much these works have or have not in common with the rich flow of children's book illustration around the world, the vitality and sense of life that they embody will reward the attention of those who see them, whether they are adults, or children, or those of that interesting age in between.

Joanna Carey

A Certain Magic

Book illustrations don't often find themselves in galleries, framed and submitted to the public gaze as independent art objects. Generally they take a more stealthy approach, quietly biding their time between the covers of a book, just waiting for what must be, for the book, a spine-tingling moment, when it is eased from the shelf and opened. And it's in that moment of opening that a certain magic takes place: a bond is made, a compact that puts the reader in a unique one-to-one relationship with the pictures. There's a scene in chapter one of *Jane Eyre* that exemplifies that intimacy. Jane, aged ten, has been banished from the family group by the fireside. As she leaves the room, she slips a book from the bookcase 'taking care that it should be one stored with pictures', and hides herself away in a curtained window seat. The book she has chosen is Bewick's *History of British Birds*, and although, as she says, 'the letterpress thereof I cared little for', she is immediately absorbed by the pictures.

> I cannot tell what sentiment haunted the quite solitary churchyard, with its inscribed headstone; its gate, its two trees, its low horizon, girdled by a broken wall, and its newly-risen crescent, attesting the hour of eventide.

> The two ships becalmed on a torpid sea, I believed to be marine phantoms.

> The fiend pinning down the thief's pack behind him, I passed over quickly: it was an object of terror.

> So was the black, horned thing seated aloof on a rock, surveying a distant crowd surrounding a gallows.

> Each picture told a story; mysterious often to my undeveloped understanding and imperfect feelings, yet ever profoundly interesting: as interesting as the tales Bessie sometimes narrated on winter evenings, when she chanced to be in good humour; and when, having brought her ironing-table to the nursery-hearth, she ... fed our eager attention with passages of love and adventure taken from old fairy tales and older ballads ...

> With Bewick on my knee, I was then happy: happy at least in my way. I feared nothing but interruption, and that came too soon.

It's worth hunting down a copy of Bewick's *History of British Birds* to see the little vignettes, or tailpieces, at the end of each chapter. They do indeed have their own stories to tell: Bewick liked to call them his 'tale pieces' because in

Thomas Bewick: tailpiece engraved for the *History of British Birds*, 1797

them he recalls incidents from his rural upbringing – memories that involve some extraordinary images. There's a 'green man' figure bursting from a tree trunk, a hanged man on a gibbet, children running wild in a graveyard and, no bigger than a postage stamp, a mysterious lobster clutching a paintbrush, and an engraved fingerprint whose whorled convolutions precisely echo the distinctive lines of Bewick's engraving technique. It's easy to see how a ten-year-old – or anyone – would be intrigued by these engravings.

Bewick, born in 1753, at Cherryburn near Newcastle, is at the start of a long line of British illustrators whose work has the power to carry the imagination way beyond the limits of the text.

To explore the development of illustration in children's books is to enter a deep dark forest – a well-worn metaphor perhaps – but in children's literature, particularly in the 19th century, the forest forms an essential backdrop, with a trail that winds in and out through the delicate tracery of Richard Doyle's fairy foliage, the crosshatched gloom of Tenniel's crepuscular oak trees, and the sinister arboreal anthropomorphism of Arthur Rackham. And meanwhile, as they say, in another part of the forest, where the light of the present day begins to filter through the canopy, there

Arthur Rackham:
'In the Forest with a Barrel' from *Rip Van Winkle*
by Washington Irving,
1905

are the benevolent boughs of E.H. Shepard's beeches in the *Winnie the Pooh* books where, as the writer Russell Davies has so aptly noted, 'the trees preside: they stand for the adult world while accommodating the fantasy'.

And it's a densely populated forest – ever since folk tales and fairy stories first emerged from the fertile undergrowth of the oral tradition, they have been written and re-written, illustrated and re-illustrated, and, in the early 19th century, the ever-increasing number of illustrated papers and periodicals meant that more and more artists were available. Many artists came to children's books having developed their drawing skills as visual reporters; many served early apprenticeships as printers and engravers; many divided their time between illustration and painting. Most knew from an early age that they wanted to be artists, and none of them seemed to perceive any barrier between books for children and books for adults. By focusing here on just a few of them, it's possible to get an idea of the diversity of talent, inspiration and invention that was channelled into the making of pictures for children's books.

Until the 18th century, apart from religious and educational material, books for children didn't really exist. Children had to make do with adult books that were deemed 'suitable' for them, and it was generally thought that they should read for instruction rather than for entertainment. But eventually children came to be recognised as individuals with their own needs. The publisher John Newbery was one of the first to recognise the commercial implications of making children's books widely available and he quickly realised the value of illustrations in attracting young readers – as Alice was to say, 100 years later, 'What is the use of a book without pictures or conversations?' So, illustrated, or 'adorned with cuts', John Newbery's books sold like hot cakes and the children's book trade began.

John Newbery's edition of *Little Goody Two-Shoes*, 1766

The 'cuts' in question, like those in the popular chapbooks of the day, were usually woodcuts. Although few in number, woefully small, and often crudely executed, at their best they were bold in design and ambitious in their narrative thrust. Engravings on metal were sometimes used but they were more expensive because they had to be printed separately from the text, whereas a woodblock could be used alongside movable type.

From John Newbery's edition of *Robinson Crusoe* by Daniel Defoe, 1766

Today, of course, modern technology makes it possible for even the merest pencil squiggle, or the most ethereal watercolour wash, to retain its eloquence in reproduction; indeed, when Edward Ardizzone's *Little Tim* books were re-published recently, the 'state of the art' scanning process not only gave a new lease of life to Ardizzone's original artwork, but also, inadvertently, to the faint, hitherto unnoticed footprints of his cat, who must have walked across the drawing-board while he worked.

But in the early days of mass production, however good, however lively an original drawing was before it was transferred to the woodblock, the success of the illustration depended heavily on the interpretative skill of the reproductive engraver. So, when Thomas Bewick developed a new technique of wood engraving at the end of the 18th century, illustration made a great leap forward.

Bewick, as a child, had taught himself to draw, even though a shortage of materials often limited him to colouring his ink drawings of birds with blackberry juice, or simply chalking on gravestones. He was apprenticed to an engraver at 14, engraving sword blades, door plates and chapbook illustrations. Perhaps it was the latter that inspired him to perfect a new technique of engraving on the end-grain of the wood (as opposed to the side); this had a denser texture which allowed a much finer line, more detail and, significantly, a subtle range of tonal variety. Bewick's work had a new and distinctive finesse – even on a tiny scale, as in the vignettes that Jane Eyre refers to, you are conscious very quickly of the subtlety of the drawing, the atmospheric use of tone and the versatility of the line.

The key to most illustrators' work is the line. Children understand the line, they respond to it instinctively and there's an interesting point at which they begin to be able to distinguish the work of one artist from another; they may not be able to tell you the name of the artist, but in many cases they can recognise the line – it's like knowing someone's handwriting. Bewick's method of engraving, which continued in use right through the Victorian age, made it possible for a line to retain something of its character in reproduction, though of course the artist was still at the mercy of the craftsman who prepared the block – not all artists could do their own engraving, like Bewick.

George Cruikshank, as an etcher, worked with a very different sort of line. Like Bewick, Cruikshank was both artist and craftsman, and he didn't need a middleman to prepare his plates. He too made an early start to his career – he was only seven when his father, Isaac, taught him to etch. And like Isaac, he worked as a caricaturist, and a visual reporter. He went on to illustrate Dickens, but it was with his etched illustrations for the first English translation of the fairy tales of the brothers Grimm (*German Popular Stories*) that he first found fame. His fluent draughtsmanship was a large part of his success as an etcher. While wood engraving involves relief printing, etching is an intaglio process: a metal plate is covered with a wax ground into which the artist draws directly with a sharp point, as with a pencil. The plate is then put in acid which etches, or bites, the exposed metal. The resulting lines are filled with ink, the surface is wiped clean and the plate is printed under great pressure that forces the ink out of the lines and on to the paper. Cruikshank could control the process at every stage; he could make any alterations he felt necessary, so the work was entirely his, retaining all the character of his original vision. *German Popular Stories* was published in 1823, in two volumes. By today's standards, when fairy tales tend to be illustrated to within an inch of their lives, these two volumes are tiny, and although (or maybe because) the illustrations are relatively few and far between, they have maximum impact. As Thackeray remarked, Cruikshank, with his background as a caricaturist, 'brought English pictorial humour and children together', but there's much more here than humour: there's real energy in these intricate compositions, and such subtlety in the dramatic groupings and the inky shadows of those firelit interiors. The figures

George Cruikshank:
from *German Popular Stories*
by the Brothers Grimm, 1823

have a mischievous, angular vitality: hands and particularly feet are expressively drawn. There's an upward rhythm throughout, and even the furniture has a restless energy – as in *Jorinda and Joringel*, where the table looks set to scuttle out of the door on cabriole legs that so comically mimic those of the startled cat.

And then there's that young man riding full tilt perched on the tail of a fox – an impossible feat, obviously, but with Cruikshank's combination of objective realism and graphic wizardry, it works – disbelief is suspended – the fox flies on. He achieves the same easy lift-off with the ogre leaping across the hills in seven-league boots, and one is reminded of the graphic skills Quentin Blake has so often called on in illustrating Roald Dahl, whose characters are frequently to be found hurtling at high speed out of open windows, airborne through no fault of their own.

David Hockney: from *Six Fairy Tales*
by the Brothers Grimm, 1970

Fairy tales have never been confined to the nursery. Far from it. In 1969 David Hockney made a series of etchings to illustrate *Grimm's Fairy Tales*. Hockney's etched line has a mesmerising austerity against which he uses

Paula Rego: *Old Mother Goose*, 1989

a rich variety of tonal effects inspired by the work of other etchers, such as Goya's use of aquatint and Morandi's painstaking crosshatching. Paula Rego's etchings also summon up the spirit of Goya in her very free interpretations of the classic nursery rhymes. Because she's clearly not addressing the very young, she's free to explore the ambiguities in these mysterious rhymes, and with her dark, almost hallucinatory imagery she offers a new reading of Mother Goose that is both gleeful and disturbing.

Although William Blake's poem 'The Tyger' must be one of the most frequently anthologised poems today, well known in almost every classroom, Blake himself had no formal education: as a child he was a startlingly unusual character whose visionary tendencies emerged at the age of four, when he saw God looking through the window. He saw angels in a tree at Peckham Rye and, according to one biographer, his father 'recognised that so strange and stormy a child must be spared the discipline of school'. So he learnt to read and write at home, and because of his precocious artistic ability studied classical drawing and at 14 entered a seven-year apprenticeship, and became a professional engraver. A visionary, painter, poet, etcher, engraver, Blake was as passionate as he was prolific and he was fierce on the subject of drawing. 'He who thinks he can engrave, or paint either without being a master of drawing is a fool. Painting is drawing on canvas, engraving is drawing on copper and nothing else.'

Only a tiny percentage of his output is specifically addressed to children, but *Songs of Innocence*, from *The Illuminated Books*, is of enormous importance. Blake felt that poetry and design were the same thing in different forms, so he created his picture poems as independent artworks, achieving on each page what so many creators of children's books strive for today: a complete integration

of words and pictures. Technically this was difficult for Blake, but with the help of his deceased brother Robert, who appeared to him in a vision, he invented a method of relief etching, which reversed the conventional process. It was a laborious business in which the text, in mirror-writing, and the (very intricate) design were painted directly on to the plate with stopping-out varnish. Acid then etched the areas around the painted line, leaving the design raised up in relief. The resulting printed line has the gentle fluency of a brush stroke, colours are soft and grainy. *Songs of Innocence* are short lyric poems which remember the intense joys of childhood and the delights of the countryside. Blake drew like an angel; he perhaps was an angel of sorts, and though much of his work is heavy with the influence of his early classical drawing, with its monumental poses, anatomical complexities and archaic gestures, the figures here are drawn with infinite tenderness and humility: repeated curves embrace the simple shapes of mothers, children, and grazing lambs, while tiny figures climb around the lettering, and dance about on distant hillsides to music you can almost hear.

William Blake: *Songs of Innocence*, 1789

It's alarming to think that Edward Lear, the 'laureate of nonsense' and one of the best known, best loved of all children's author-illustrators, fell into that role almost by accident. The youngest of 21 children, Lear decided to be an artist after seeing some paintings by Turner. At 16 he began to earn a living as an artist, making among other things 'morbid disease drawing for hospitals and certain doctors of physic'. He then became an ornithological draughtsman, and at 18 had a success with a book about parrots – as a result of which he was commissioned to make drawings at a private menagerie on the estate of the Earl of Derby. Whilst there, he began entertaining the many

William Blake: 'What is Man!'
from *For Children: The Gates of Paradise*,
1793

Edward Lear: 'Queeriflora Babyöides'
from *Laughable Lyrics: A Fourth Book of
Nonsense Poems, Songs, Botany, Music etc.*
1877

were enchanting, but Tenniel's original black and white vision has a powerful immutability and has never really been surpassed. Perhaps Tenniel's work at *Punch* magazine as political cartoonist and his familiarity with parliamentary goings-on at Westminster gave him an insight, not just into the bewildering illogicalities of the text but also the extravagant surreal imagery. Remarkably unaffected by the fact that his father had accidentally blinded him in one eye with a fencing foil, Tenniel drew his designs directly on to the woodblocks, which would then be engraved by the famous Dalziel brothers.

John Tenniel: The Mock Turtle
and the Gryphon with Alice,
from *Alice's Adventures in Wonderland*
by Lewis Carroll, 1865

children of the house, unleashing a torrent of nonsensical rhymes and pictures. Clattering across the page in perpetual motion, with a spur-of-the-moment informality, Lear's exuberantly uninhibited illustrations are surely the first to express the economy and spontaneity that is the hallmark of so many of today's illustrators. He scarcely bothers with backgrounds; the figures, almost always pictured in eloquent attitudes of spiralling absurdity, have shapeless roly-poly bodies with elegantly tapering extremities and huge faces big enough to accommodate extravagant facial expressions. But although he takes liberties with the human form, Lear's animals and birds, however loosely drawn, are sharply observed. There's something about Lear, the innocence of his careless raptures and his compact picture/poem format, that recalls William Blake – and among the looping, drooping foliage of the 'nonsense botany', Blake's little baby in a chrysalis, guarded by a caterpillar on a leaf, wouldn't look out of place alongside Lear's 'Queeriflora Babyöides'.

The fashion for nonsense extended over a long period, and Lewis Carroll's *Alice's Adventures in Wonderland* (1865) didn't appear until 20 years after Lear's *Book of Nonsense*. Carroll had intended to illustrate *Alice* himself, but he was persuaded not to, and Tenniel was chosen on the strength of his illustrations to Aesop. Since then *Alice* has become a sort of illustrators' Everest – literally hundreds of attempts have been made by an astonishing diversity of artists that includes Marie Laurençin, W. Heath Robinson, Mabel Lucie Attwell, Salvador Dali and Mervyn Peake. One of the first, and one of the very best, was Arthur Rackham. His version appeared 42 years after Tenniel; by then new printing technology made it possible for him combine his sinuous witchy line with subtle, muted colour. The results

However fanciful Carroll's demands on his imagination – the Gryphon, the Cheshire-Cat, the Frog-Footman – Tenniel drew with unfailing gravitas and authority: he drew the Mock Turtle complete with calf's head (in accordance with Mrs Beeton's recipe for mock turtle soup in her 1861 *Book of Household Management*). He drew the Jabberwock, the Knitting Sheep and the Rocking-horse-fly all with the same straight-faced realism, although he refused even to attempt drawing a wasp in a wig – which, he said, 'was quite beyond the appliances of art.' (Lear, however, might have managed it – see his wasp playing the flute in a morning cap.)

John Tenniel: The Rocking-horse-fly,
from *Through the Looking-Glass*
by Lewis Carroll, 1872

Edward Lear: The
Worrying Whizzing
Wasp, from *Twenty-
Six Nonsense Rhymes
and Pictures*, 1872

There are many incidents in the fairy tales that might well be considered 'beyond the appliances of art.' Scenes like the ugly sisters chopping their toes off to fit the glass slipper, the wicked stepmother dancing herself to death in red-hot iron shoes, and the dreadful carnage in *Red Riding Hood*, make you realise the extraordinary demands made of illustrators, and the resourcefulness with which they cope. In recent times Michael Foreman used a *trompe l'oeil* effect to suggest the horror in Brian Alderson's translation of *Fitcher's Bird*, and Quentin Blake borrowed an image from a Thurber cartoon to deal with the rather unexpected beheading scene in Roald Dahl's version of *Cinderella*.

The Victorians had strong stomachs for gruesome illustrations, but even so the British publishers of *Little Poucet*, from the tales of Perrault, censored Doré's very explicit 1882 engraving of the ogre just about to slit the throats of his little daughters.

Walter Crane, however, managed to bring a humorous touch to that ugly scene in *The Frog Prince* when the princess angrily throws the frog at the wall in the royal bedchamber and, against the elegant drapes of the four-poster, in a cloud of something resembling ectoplasm, the splattered, goggle-eyed frog cuts some comical capers before completing his princely metamorphosis.

Walter Crane: *The Frog Prince*, 1874

Aged 13, Crane had been apprenticed to an engraver and at 18 was taken up by Edmund Evans, the man who revolutionised colour printing in the latter part of the 19th century. Under Evans, Crane, Randolph Caldecott and Kate Greenaway all became, in their very different ways, leading creators of picture books. Crane was a very fine and versatile draughtsman but his work, at its height, is notable above all for the sophistication of the design. A leading figure in the Arts and Crafts movement, he was, like so many artists at that time, strongly influenced by the work of the Japanese printmakers. His picture books abound with black outlines, richly patterned surfaces and flattened perspective. 'Children prefer well defined forms and bright frank colour,' he said, 'they don't want to bother with three dimensions'. He seemed almost to anticipate the style of the cartoon strip by dividing the page up into boxes, but although there's always a lot of action in his pictures, there's not a lot of movement – the black line, like the leaded line in a stained-glass window, tends to seize the figures and immobilise them, making them part of the overall pattern.

Randolph Caldecott: *R. Caldecott's Picture Book No.2*, 1885

Where Crane was mannered and purposely stylised, Randolph Caldecott was spontaneous and joyful. Having worked as a visual reporter on *The Graphic*, he was able to draw with speed and economy and, with his racy calligraphic style, he prided himself on being a master of 'leaving things out', though one thing he handed down to today's picture book artists was his habit of subtly extending the narrative with a sprinkling of visual clues to things beyond the scope of the text – a concept that the writer Philip Pullman has identified as the graphic equivalent of 'counterpoint'. It is a concept that John Burningham wittily took to its logical conclusion in *Time to Get out of the Bath, Shirley*, where on one page Mum is droning on in monochrome about tidying up, apparently oblivious to the fact that on the opposite page Shirley has escaped down the plughole to a life of colour and adventure.

The critic John Ruskin was an influential figure in the world of children's books. His career spanned the whole of the 19th century: he admired Bewick, and he lavished praise on Cruikshank, comparing him to Rembrandt. Ruskin's enthusiasm was widespread – he chose the fairy painter Richard Doyle to illustrate his own book, *The King of the Golden River*, and he was as keen on the informal nonsense of Edward Lear as he was on the idealised reality of Kate Greenaway, which he thought would have an improving effect on society. Greenaway, with Ruskin's support, had enormous success, but although her illustrations are highly decorative, light and spacious, the children she draws have a curious listlessness – perhaps something to do with the huge mob-caps and Regency costumes they are obliged to wear.

Beatrix Potter: *The Tailor of Gloucester*, 1903

Beatrix Potter: *The Tale of Peter Rabbit*, 1903

How much more convincing those costumes are on Beatrix Potter's mice in *The Tailor of Gloucester*! Although there were some talking animals in Victorian times, it wasn't until the 20th century that anthropomorphism became endemic in children's books. But while Potter's characters wear clothes and act out little dramas, they always remain true to their animal selves. The way Peter Rabbit puts his head back to pull and nibble at his food is very realistically captured, and wittily echoed when he lifts his chin to have his coat buttoned by his mother. The drawing is faultless because Potter knew her subject inside out – literally – for, as children with a passion for natural history, she and her brother kept all sorts of small creatures as pets. They drew and painted them constantly, sketching any available corpses before skinning them for further research, then boiling them up in order to retrieve the skeletons. Potter's first book grew from an illustrated letter she wrote to a child, so even from the start the words sat naturally with the pictures, and she always worked on a small scale to suit the size of a child's hand. Potter's drawing has a natural honesty. She never exaggerates, never distorts, the line is constantly alert to the slightest twitch of a whisker, and she had a fine watercolour technique that makes no concessions to young readers. In his autobiography, *Surprised by Joy*, the author C.S. Lewis writes of the way *Squirrel Nutkin* affected his whole life:

It troubled me with what I can only describe as 'the Idea of Autumn'. It sounds fantastic to say that one can be enamoured of a season, but that is something like what happened . . . the experience was one of intense desire. And one went back to the book, not to gratify the desire, but to re-awake it. It was something quite different from ordinary life and even from ordinary pleasure; something, as they would now say, 'in another dimension'.

E.H.Shepard: from *The House at Pooh Corner* by A.A. Milne, 1928

While Potter gave animals human characteristics, E.H. Shepard achieved a sort of double anthropomorphic triumph: the creatures he breathed life into were not just animals, but shabby old toy animals. Shepard drew obsessively throughout his life. As a schoolboy he drew on the back of his Latin homework, and attended Saturday Art Classes at Heatherley's before winning a scholarship to the Royal Academy Schools. He illustrated all his letters, kept copious sketchbooks during his war service and worked as a prolific cartoonist for *Punch*.

He was constantly drawing people and when he started work on *Pooh*, his talent for capturing expressive attitudes and gestures – indeed all the subtleties of body language – worked equally well when the body in question was stuffed with kapok. You can tell exactly what that bear is thinking, even from behind. It's all in the precise tilt of his head, the slight droop of his shoulder, and there's always something rather touchingly awkward about his arms, as if he doesn't quite know how to hold them.

E.H.Shepard: from *The House at Pooh Corner* by A.A. Milne, 1928

Shepard had a magic touch; he drew with freshness and simplicity, and an understated wit. Not many artists can carry off the trick of bringing toys to life without falling prey to sentimentality. William Nicholson did it dashingly in *Clever Bill* (1928). Quentin Blake does it by giving his Clown the gift of mime, and Emma Chichester Clark's Blue Kangaroo finds his independent mobility in theatrical moonlight.

One of the best known and most influential illustrators of the 20th century was Edward Ardizzone, whose style had its roots in the traditions of Hogarth, Rowlandson and Daumier, and whose work anticipated much of what was to come. There are many illustrators like Charlotte Voake and Patrick Benson for whom Ardizzone's buoyant line is clearly a principal source of inspiration.

Edward Ardizzone: *Sketches for Friends*, 2000

Edward Ardizzone: *Tim's Friend Towser*, 1956

Ardizzone is probably best remembered for his *Tim and Lucy* books. He drew constantly – according to his daughter Christianna, who was the inspiration for the Lucy character, he drew on the backs of cigarette packets, or any old scrap of paper, drawing not from life but from what he remembered having seen a little earlier. He was a generous communicator in his drawings – you always get a vivid sense of place, and although the pictures are packed with information, the detail is never fussy or laboured, gestures and facial expressions, however breezily suggested, are eloquent and, with vigorous use of watercolour and a classical approach to the laws of composition, his illustrations, however dramatic, always manage to convey an underlying sense of security and well-being. He won the Kate Greenaway medal in 1956, and in a witty response to the dramatic difference between his style and Greenaway's, he drew a picture of himself 'in the mantle of Kate Greenaway' looking rather like Queen Victoria, in a bonnet.

In addition to all his picture books Ardizzone was much in demand for his black and white line drawings for books by a vast array of authors, from Dickens and J.M. Barrie to Eleanor Farjeon and Philippa Pearce.

Another versatile artist renowned for his work both in colour and in line was Charles Keeping. His powerful, muscular line drawings for Edward Blishen and Leon Garfield's retellings of Greek myths, *The God Beneath the Sea*, are some of the most strikingly innovative black and white illustrations of that period.

Recent years have seen a decline in black and white illustration. Sadly, where once they created little oases of visual interest, today line drawings are no longer *de rigueur* in children's novels. Classics and old favourites fare better however, and Tony Ross has brilliantly re-illustrated some old favourites like *Just William* and *Pippi Longstocking*. In an earlier era, Harry Potter would surely have had an illustrator, but there's a tendency now for fictional characters to get their visual identity from the world of film and television, though, conversely, Alan Lee's stunning illustrations for Tolkien have played an important part in the making of the recent film *The Lord of the Rings*.

Alan Lee: from *The Lord of the Rings* by J.R.R.Tolkien, 1991

Brian Wildsmith: *The Owl and the Woodpecker*, 1971

In the 1960s technological advances in four-colour half-tone printing brought a dramatic explosion of light and colour to the world of illustration and new horizons opened up for the picture book, which came to be seen as an art object in its own right. Free now of so many of the constraints and limitations in terms of reproduction, artists were able to employ a much wider range of media, and picture books became bolder and brighter than ever before. Brian Wildsmith, for instance, one of the most noticeable picture book artists of this time, gave his images an unprecedented painterly quality – so much so that children were reported as wanting to lick them. Subject-matter expanded dramatically, as did perceived age limits, and picture books began to be, as they are now, the subject of widespread critical and even scholarly appraisal. In addition to their popularity in homes and libraries, teachers began to be aware of their value in the classroom.

To look in a children's bookshop is to be astonished by the rich diversity of the different categories on offer. 'Babies need books' is a well known cry today and there's a proliferation of 'first books', books for toddlers and pre-school children. Shirley Hughes, Helen Oxenbury, John Burningham and the Ahlbergs are just a few of those who have created an abundance of books that explore the everyday textures of life from a child's point of view. But this is a relatively recent phenomenon – as Shirley Hughes said, talking about her work in an interview in *The Guardian*, 'You won't believe this, but in the 1960s there were hardly any books about what small children did all day.'

Lucy tips all her plastic animals out of their box and she and Tom make them march across the floor, two by two.

Shirley Hughes: *Lucy & Tom's 1.2.3.*, 1987

Drawing on her own experience of family life, *Lucy and Tom's Day* was just the first of Shirley Hughes' ever popular succession of books that affectionately chronicle the everyday life of children – children living in towns, children living in flats, playing indoors, going to the shops, playing in parks, and enjoying, in a way that would have warmed the heart of William Blake, the pleasures of the countryside. Hughes, like so many others, started her illustrating career working in black and white – in those pre-1960 days you couldn't even use a wash – all tonality had to be created with line, so illustrators really had to be able to draw. Hughes draws with an inquisitive, descriptive line that leaves no stone unturned in the search for form, substance and familiar detail, and she combines this with a watercolour technique that is both robust and sensitive.

Shirley Hughes: *Lucy & Tom's 1.2.3.*, 1987

The writer Francis Spufford had Shirley Hughes' books as a child, and, as he recalls in his recent memoir about the power of childhood reading:

> . . . the ordinary scenes of Lucy and Tom's day affected me almost viscerally. The little red and blue train Tom played with seemed to be the essence of toy . . . the smeech of treacle on Tom's face at teatime had in it, in concentrated form, the comedy of disorder, the hilarity of things being out of place. *Lucy and Tom's Day* didn't bring in a single element I couldn't recognise from my own life.

Janet and Allan Ahlberg: *Peepo*, 1981

The line between everyday life and the world of make-believe is enchantingly blurred in Janet Ahlberg's illustrations. Ahlberg brought a new simplicity to the way children are portrayed, drawing faces with little more than a line, two dots and a rosy blush. Her line has an infectious vitality and her characters, whether from the real world, or the world of fairytale, combine an airy innocence with a wicked sense of humour. And in her wonderfully lived-in interiors, she invests even the most mundane household objects, such as teapots, bedroom slippers, mangles and chamber pots, with a reassuring sense of affectionate nostalgia.

The children Helen Oxenbury draws have a much more contemporary feel. And it's the robust reality of the children that heightens the fantasy element in her book *We're All Going on a Bear Hunt*. This is a wonderful evocation of a light-hearted, imaginative family outing in the countryside to look for a bear – and a breathless stampede back to the house when they find one. There are four children (the eldest is clearly the prototype for Oxenbury's version of *Alice's Adventures in Wonderland*, which she set in the present day) and their excitable mood swings are reflected in alternating pages of black and white line drawings and atmospheric, beautifully modulated watercolours.

Family life in the 21st century is vigorously portrayed in Lauren Child's boldly inventive spreads. With scrawly drawings, cartoony figures, and unruly, kaleidoscopic collages that sample, rather as pop music does, bits and pieces from all over the place, she effortlessly juggles fabrics, wallpapers, photographic images and twirling typography. On the face of it, Lauren Child doesn't have a lot in common with Walter Crane, but it was Crane who declared that 'children don't want to bother with three dimensions', and he might well have approved of the way Child makes use of bold black lines, flat colours and plenty of surface pattern in her entertainingly chaotic interiors. The general effect is a democratic flattening of the perspective that gives equal importance to everything on the page, rather as children do in their drawings. It's a style that both reflects and boldly grapples with the bewildering abundance of visual material that surrounds us today. Everything around us, it seems, now strives to have an arresting visual presence – everything is illustrated – cereal packets, sweet wrappers, carrier bags, T-shirts; buses and taxis are swathed in advertisements, and there's always a graffiti artist ready to fill in the odd blank wall.

Helen Oxenbury: from *We're All Going on a Bear Hunt* by Michael Rosen, 1989

Humour has always played a major role in children's books: the first illustrators were caricaturists and, in line with that tradition, Quentin Blake was successfully submitting cartoons to *Punch* when he was still a schoolboy. But although Quentin Blake, John Burningham and Raymond Briggs all originally made their mark as humorous artists, they all reach out to areas far beyond the realms of comedy. While Blake can make you laugh out loud with a single expressive flourish of his scratchy nib, he can just as easily switch the mood to one of quiet reflection, as in *The Green Ship*, in which a clump of trees becomes a metaphor for the passage of time; or his book *Clown* which has no words at all, but tells a moving, life-affirming story entirely through the urgent, eloquent gestures of its eponymous hero, an outgrown toy clown who has to rebuild his life after being thrown out with the rubbish.

There's a similar breadth of vision in the work of John Burningham. Familiarity with the expressive economy of his sparse line, and his wonderfully deadpan, oblique humour does nothing to prepare you for the ravishingly beautiful effect of the sumptuous photographic images in *Cloudland*, against which the superimposed paper cut-outs of flying children have such a vulnerable, ephemeral quality.

Flight is a recurring theme in children's books, and Raymond Briggs' Snowman, who takes a little boy on an enchanting journey in the night sky, has become a legendary figure. Working in his customary comic strip format, Briggs' drawings of the little boy in his winceyette pyjamas are observed with utmost tenderness, and magically enhanced by the tactile quality of the pencil and coloured crayon that so perfectly suggests both the textures of the child's immediate world, and the power of his imagination.

In addition to this most gentle of fantasies, Briggs has used the comic strip format to explore a vast range of territories – from high comedy and poignant social comment to fierce political satire. Like Michael Foreman, whose book *War Game* so movingly chronicles in pictures the lives – and deaths – of three soldiers in the First World War, Briggs isn't afraid to tackle difficult subjects, like war, illness and death. He sees no age limits and his easy-to-read pictures make these books accessible at almost all levels of understanding.

Another artist with a natural affinity for the comic strip and the infinite variety of its story-telling possibilities is Colin McNaughton. Steeped in popular culture, and often densely populated with all sorts of familiar comic characters, his work is an engaging combination of

Helen Oxenbury: from *Alice's Adventures in Wonderland* by Lewis Carroll, 1999

Colin McNaughton: *Have You Seen Who's Just Moved in Next Door to Us?*, 1991

rowdy slapstick humour and graphic finesse; but *Watch Out for the Giant Killers* shows him in a sensitive thought-provoking 'green' mode, with vast jungle-scapes and generous attention to detail.

'Exuberant' is perhaps an overused word in connection with children's book illustrations, but it's unavoidable in the case of Babette Cole. In common with most of the artists here, she writes her own stories, from feminist fairy tales to shaggy-dog stories, and a wide range of uninhibited books that explore areas of non-fiction that are traditionally handled in a less exuberant, less satirical way.

In *Mummy Laid an Egg* two children explain to their embarrassed parents the mechanics of human reproduction using their own crudely schematic drawings. The book is hugely funny and graphically explicit – though at so many removes from reality, not alarmingly so. Cole's technical skill is as wide ranging as her satire, and she adapts it accordingly. Often she draws with a slapdash vitality, with frequent use of exclamatory emphasis. But when the mood changes, the line has a mischievous delicacy and she can bring a rare luminosity to her watercolours.

In total contrast to Babette Cole's reckless exuberance, Posy Simmonds' work is notable for the discipline and fine tuning of the page design. Simmonds made her name with a strip cartoon in *The Guardian*. Her work combines a razor-sharp wit with sly social observation and immaculate drawing skills that allow her to capture the significance of the slightest gesture or the merest little sideways glance. She backs up her relentlessly accurate character assessments with merciless attention to telling details like shoes, hemlines, handbags and, on a broader scale, with domestic interiors where, as in *Gemma Bovery*, she never misses an opportunity to eye up the furniture and fittings. Children and animals are drawn with a slightly more forgiving line.

There's a similar wit and precision in Fritz Wegner's work. He draws with a wiry spring-loaded line, full of energy, and perfectly controlled with a celebratory enjoyment of detail and an easy way with formal flourishes and decorative devices and hand-lettering. Always there is a sense of spatial awareness which gives great depth to his illustrations; figures are brilliantly drawn and he excels at crowd scenes: even on the smallest scale, each figure has an expressive individuality.

Babette Cole: *Lady Lupin's Book of Etiquette*, 2001

While Wegner's drawings define perfectly the meaning of the words 'to illustrate' which is to illuminate, or make clear, Anthony Browne's work has an intriguing obfuscatory quality, which famously invites and rewards repeated investigation.

Appealing across a wide range, and laced with subtle humour, arcane references and myriad visual and psychological puzzles, Browne's numerous books abound in themes of identity, disguise and metamorphosis, and the work is frequently inspired by images from the world of fine art, particularly in the realms of Dada and Surrealism. His unique, close-toned, meticulously finished style has a mysterious dream-like intensity. In *Voices in the Park*, where the spirit of Magritte is evoked, the subtle dynamics of the relationships between the characters in the story are teasingly explored in illustrations that seamlessly interweave the mundane with the magical.

An artist with a very different take on the modernist conventions of the 20th century is David McKee. Flattening his world up against the picture plane in a tiny perspective

Fritz Wegner: from *The Tale of the Turnip* retold by Brian Alderson, 1999

only millimetres deep, he plays some vertiginous tricks on the reader, exploiting or paying homage to artists such as Klee and Matisse. In *Charlotte's Piggy Bank* there's an Escher-like confusion of staircases, and an aerial viewpoint that turns everything topsy-turvy. Full of jokes, puns and mischievous detail, these pictures are easy to read and fun to explore at more than one level of comprehension.

The artist Angela Barrett has an even more intimate relationship with earlier tradition, although in a manner which, in its subtle distortions, is less conventional than

might at first appear. In *Snow White*, the deceptive formality of the composition gives way to a beguiling manipulation of space and perspective. The book becomes an enchanting laptop theatre; conspiring with the angles made when the page turns, the pictures create an illusory depth and the eye is drawn to arresting details further and further upstage. Figures, which manage to have both a tangible reality and an ethereal otherworldliness, are exquisitely drawn, often in profile in the manner of Renaissance portraits, and everywhere there is intriguing use of symbolism: a bird,

Anthony Browne: *Voices in the Park*, 1998

a jewel, an empty nest, a petal, everything is richly imbued with meaning, nothing is merely ornamental or serendipitous. When the prince has rescued Snow White from what must be the definitive fairytale forest, the mood changes dramatically and at the end a back view of the celebratory throng has the quality of a *fête champêtre*, summoning up the spirit of Watteau perhaps, or Fragonard.

Nicola Bayley's close-knit compositions have a similar intensity. Much of Bayley's work is on a very small scale,

often almost that of a miniaturist, and looking through a magnifying glass you can see that she has a meticulous pointilliste technique: like tiny coals glowing in a furnace, little dots of pigment jostle each other, creating intense energy, or melding together in diffused areas of colour with a sumptuous enamelled effect. Cats appear frequently in Bayley's work – her titles include *Patchwork Cat*, *The Necessary Cat* and *Katje, The Windmill Cat* – and her technique gives a heightened reality to the rich and varied

David McKee: *Charlotte's Piggy Bank*, 1996

Nicola Bayley: from *The Mousehole Cat* by Antonia Barber,1990

textures of their fur. In *The Mousehole Cat*, the sinuous, serpentine movements of the Storm Cat are strongly reminiscent of *Orlando*, Kathleen Hale's famous marmalade cat, and the stippled textures of Bayley's paintings seem to echo the grainy textural effect of Hale's bold lithographs, which were such a distinctive feature of the early Puffin books in the 1930s and '40s.

Kathleen Hale: *Orlando the Marmalade Cat: His Silver Wedding*, 1944

While Angela Barrett and Nicola Bayley are representative of artists still working in traditional painting techniques, John Lawrence is a striking example of that small number of artists still making effective use of the old engraving methods, though Lawrence's work today will probably more often be cut on vinyl than on wood. With a lively rhythmic quality throughout, Lawrence's bold, highly-charged designs have a powerful presence on the page and the strong narrative element is richly interwoven with subtle notes of humour which provide yet another link with Bewick.

It's clear that illustration today, alongside vast areas of innovation and ever-inventive ways of integrating text and image, still incorporates a wealth of traditional skills and influences. Draughtsmanship – often referred to in hushed terms as an endangered art – is clearly alive and well, and ranges here from the freedom and spontaneity of Quentin Blake, through the freewheeling calligraphy of Charlotte

John Lawrence: from *A New Treasury of Poetry*, selected and introduced by Neil Philip, 1990

Voake and the gentle authority of Michael Foreman, to the seductive detail and dramatic discipline of Stephen Biesty, whose heightened reality has almost literally brought a new dimension to the world of non-fiction.

Illustrations in books can only ever be as good as the technology that reproduces them, and in the early days the vision of the artist was not always matched by the capabilities of the printer. But such is the technology available today that everything can be electronically scanned and printed in the same way, whatever the nature of the original – whether it's a computer generated line drawing, a sketch done with a quill pen, an atmospheric landscape whose impact depends on the subtle luminosity of watercolour washes, or an evocative collage made from the contents of a wastepaper basket.

Illustration today is exciting and varied as never before, and the exhibition to which this book is a companion offers a unique chance to experience at first hand the physical presence of the original artwork, to see the very textures of the work, to get a sense of how these images have been created, and above all to get an idea of the surprisingly different way each artist approaches the business of illustrating a book. And, at a time when there's evidence in the arts of a growing appetite for story and, in certain areas, a return to representational work, this exhibition is a chance to celebrate an ancient art from which narrative has never been dismissed.

Quentin Blake: *The Laureate's Party*, 2000

Essay illustration sources

Janet and Allan Ahlberg: *Peepo*, first published by Viking, 1981 © Janet and Allan Ahlberg, 1981

Edward Ardizzone: *Tim's Friend Towser*, first published by Oxford University Press, 1956 © Estate of Edward Ardizzone, 2000

Edward Ardizzone: *Sketches for Friends*, first published by John Murray (Publishers) Ltd, 2000 © Estate of Edward Ardizzone, 2000

Nicola Bayley: *The Mousehole Cat* by Antonia Barber, first published by Walker Books, 1990 © Nicola Bayley

Thomas Bewick: A tailpiece engraved for the *History of British Birds* (two volumes published 1797 and 1804)

Quentin Blake: *The Laureate's Party* first published by Red Fox, 2000 © Quentin Blake

William Blake: *Songs of Innocence*, 1789 © The William Blake Trust

William Blake: *What is Man!* from *For Children: The Gates of Paradise*, 1793 © The William Blake Trust

Anthony Browne: *Voices in the Park*, first published by Doubleday a division of Transworld Publishers, 1998 © A.E.T. Browne and Partners, 1998

Randolph Caldecott: *R. Caldecott's Picture Book No.2*, published by Frederick Warne Co., 1904

Babette Cole: *Lady Lupin's Book of Etiquette*, first published by Hamish Hamilton, 2001 © Babette Cole

Walter Crane: *The Frog Prince*, 1874, reproduced by kind permission of Hornby Library, Liverpool City Libraries

George Cruikshank: The Golden Bird from *German Popular Stories by the Brothers Grimm*, published London, 1823

Kathleen Hale: *Orlando the Marmalade Cat: His Silver Wedding*, first published by Country Life, 1944 © Estate of Kathleen Hale

David Hockney: The Enchantress with the Baby Rapunzel from *Six Fairy Tales from the Brothers Grimm: Rapunzel*, Petersburg Press, 1970

Shirley Hughes: *Lucy & Tom's 1.2.3.*, first published by Victor Gollancz Ltd, 1987 © Shirley Hughes

Shirley Hughes: *Rhymes for Annie Rose*, first published by The Bodley Head, 1995 © Shirley Hughes

John Lawrence: *A New Treasury of Poetry* selected and introduced by Neil Philip, Blackie, 1990

Edward Lear: The Worrying Whizzing Wasp from *Twenty-Six Nonsense Rhymes and Pictures*, 1872

Edward Lear: Queeriflora Babÿoïdes, from *Laughable Lyrics: A Fourth Books of Nonsense Poems, Songs, Botany, etc.*, 1877

Alan Lee: *The Lord of the Rings* by J.R.R.Tolkien, published by HarperCollins, 1991 © Alan Lee

David McKee: *Charlotte's Piggy Bank*, first published by Andersen Press, 1996 © David McKee

Colin McNaughton: *Have you Seen who's Just Moved in Next Door to Us?*, first published by Walker Books, 1991 © Colin McNaughton

Helen Oxenbury: *We're all Going on a Bear Hunt* by Michael Rosen, first published by Walker Books, 1989 © Helen Oxenbury

Helen Oxenbury: *Alice's Adventures in Wonderland* by Lewis Carroll, first published by Walker Books, 2001 © Helen Oxenbury

Beatrix Potter: *The Tailor of Gloucester*, first published by Frederick Warne & Co., 1903 © Frederick Warne & Co., 1903, 1987, 2002

Beatrix Potter: *The Tale of Peter Rabbit*, first published by Frederick Warne & Co., 1903 © Frederick Warne & Co., 1903, 1987, 2002

Arthur Rackham: In the Forest with a Barrel from *Rip Van Winkle* by Washington Irving, 1905, collection The Fine Art Society, London, reproduced with the kind permission of the Rackham family/Bridgeman Art Library

Paula Rego: *Old Mother Goose*, etching and aquatint, 1989 © Paula Rego

E.H.Shepard: *The House at Pooh Corner* by A.A.Milne, first published, 1928 © line illustrations by Ernest H. Shepard copyright under the Berne Convention

John Tenniel: The Mock Turtle and The Gryphon with Alice from *Alice's Adventures in Wonderland* by Lewis Carroll, first published 1865

John Tenniel: the Rocking-horse-fly from *Through the Looking-Glass* by Lewis Carroll, first published 1872

Fritz Wegner: *The Tale of the Turnip* retold by Brian Alderson, first published by Walker Books, 1999 © Fritz Wegner

Brian Wildsmith: *The Owl and the Woodpecker*, first published by Oxford University Press, 1971 © Brian Wildsmith

Anon: from *The History of Little Goody Two-Shoes*, J. Newbery, 1766 (from *Books for Keeps*, no.104, May 1997)

Anon: from *Robinson Crusoe*, J. Newbery, 1766 (from *Books for Keeps*, no.104, May 1997)

The artists' illustrations

Angela Barrett: *Candide or Optimism* by Voltaire, Libanus Press, 1996, illustration © Angela Barrett

Angela Barrett: *Snow White* by Josephine Poole, first published in Britain by Red Fox, 1991, illustration © Angela Barrett; text © Josephine Poole

Patrick Benson: *The MinPins* by Roald Dahl, first published in Britain by Jonathan Cape, 1991, illustration © Patrick Benson; text © Roald Dahl

Patrick Benson: *The Lord Fish* by Walter de la Mare, first published in Britain by Walker Books, 1997, illustration © Patrick Benson; text © Estate of Walter de la Mare

Patrick Benson: *The Sea-Thing Child* by Russell Hoban, first published in Britain by Walker Books, 1999, illustration © Patrick Benson; text © Russell Hoban

Stephen Biesty: *Incredible Cross-Sections* by Richard Platt, first published in Britain by Dorling Kindersley, 1992 © Stephen Biesty

Stephen Biesty: *Man-of-War* by Richard Platt, first published in Britain by Dorling Kindersley, 1993 © Stephen Biesty

Stephen Biesty: *Incredible Explosions* by Richard Platt, first published in Britain by Dorling Kindersley, 1996 © Stephen Biesty

Quentin Blake: *The BFG* by Roald Dahl, first published in Britain by Jonathan Cape, 1982, illustration © Quentin Blake, text © Estate of Roald Dahl

Quentin Blake: *Quentin Blake's ABC*, first published in Britain by Jonathan Cape, 1989 © Quentin Blake

Quentin Blake: *Ten Frogs*, first published in Britain by Pavilion Books, 1998 © Quentin Blake

Quentin Blake: *The Green Ship*, first published in Britain by Jonathan Cape, 1998 © Quentin Blake

Raymond Briggs: *When the Wind Blows*, first published in Britain by Hamish Hamilton, 1982 © Raymond Briggs

Raymond Briggs: *Ethel & Ernest*, first published in Britain by Jonathan Cape, 1998 © Raymond Briggs

Raymond Briggs: *Ug: Boy Genius of the Stone Age*, first published in Britain by Jonathan Cape, 2001 © Raymond Briggs

John Burningham: *Aldo*, first published in Britain by Jonathan Cape, 1991 © John Burningham

John Burningham: *Cloudland*, first published in Britain by Jonathan Cape, 1996 © John Burningham

John Burningham: *Whadayamean*, first published in Britain by Jonathan Cape, 1999 © John Burningham

Emma Chichester Clark: *It was You, Blue Kangaroo!*, first published in Britain by Andersen Press, 2000 © Emma Chichester Clark

Emma Chichester Clark: *Enchantment: Fairy Tales, Ghost Stories and Tales of Wonder* selected by Kevin Crossley-Holland, first published in Britain by Orion, 2000, illustration © Emma Chichester Clark, text © Kevin Crossley-Holland

Emma Chichester Clark: *No More Kissing!*, first published in Britain by Andersen Press, 2001 © Emma Chichester Clark

Lauren Child: *I Will not Ever Never Eat a Tomato*, first published in Britain by Orchard Books, 2000 © Lauren Child

Lauren Child: *My Uncle is a Hunkle says Clarice Bean*, first published in Britain by Orchard Books, 2000 © Lauren Child

Lauren Child: *Clarice Bean, That's Me!*, first published in Britain by Orchard Books, 1999 © Lauren Child

Sara Fanelli: *Dog's Life*, first published in Britain by Heinemann Young Books, 1998 © Sara Fanelli

Sara Fanelli: *Dear Diary*, first published in Britain by Walker Books, 2000 © Sara Fanelli

Sara Fanelli: *Mythological Creatures*, first published in Britain by Macmillan, 2002 © Sara Fanelli

Michael Foreman: *Seasons of Splendour: Tales, Myths and Legends of India* by Madhur Jaffrey, first published in Britain by Hodder and Stoughton, 1985 © Michael Foreman

Michael Foreman: *War Boy: A Country Childhood*, first published in Britain by Pavilion Books Ltd, 1989 © Michael Foreman

Michael Foreman: *War Game*, first published in Britain by Pavilion Books Ltd, 1993 © Michael Foreman

Tony Ross: *I Want My Potty*, first published in Britain by HarperCollins, 1986 © Tony Ross

Tony Ross: *Susan Laughs* by Jeanne Willis, first published in Britain by Andersen Press, 1999, illustration © Tony Ross; text © Jeanne Willis

Tony Ross: *I Want to be a Cowgirl* by Jeanne Willis, first published in Britain by Andersen Press, 2001, illustration © Tony Ross; text © Jeanne Willis

Posy Simmonds: *Fred*, first published in Britain by Jonathan Cape, 1987 © Posy Simmonds

Posy Simmonds: *Gemma Bovery*, published in Britain by Jonathan Cape, 1999 © Posy Simmonds

Charlotte Voake: *The Best of Aesop's Fables* retold by Margaret Clark, first published in Britain by Walker Books, 1990, illustration © Charlotte Voake; text © Margaret Clark

Charlotte Voake: *Alphabet Adventure*, first published in the Britain by Jonathan Cape, 1999 © Charlotte Voake

THE ARTISTS

Angela Barrett

Born 1955.
Studied at Thurrock
Technical College,
Maidstone School
of Art and the
Royal College of Art,
London.

I left school at fifteen. My parents really didn't want me to go to art school. They tried to make me do a secretarial course but I managed to move sideways from that into retail display (window dressing) and from there to illustration. In the end, I spent eight years at art school.

I've got two sorts of drawing. I draw passionately all over paper tablecloths, napkins and backs of envelopes. But drawings like that are difficult to convert into anything useful. Sketch books are different, important to me. So I can jot down ideas on the spur of the moment that probably wouldn't come back to me otherwise – dreams, and other things that pass fleetingly through my mind. I use a camera quite a lot, for purposes of composition, but not for the people. People in photographs just don't look like my people. My people aren't exactly realistic. I distort them. I draw them again and again. I'm not happy really until they are out of proportion. It's something to do with the way I try to show a sense of heightened emotion. And for the same reason, I take liberties with perspective.

I don't use models, but I frequently draw myself in the mirror. If you look at Joan of Arc, that's me, imagining what it's like to be burnt at the stake at the age of eighteen. I had to tone it down though. Strangely, my editor thought I looked too unhappy. I've recently been illustrating a book about Mary Shelley. When I reached the bit where Mary Wollstonecraft has died of puerperal fever, I got out all my old dolls and I drew myself as William Godwin standing at her bedside holding the new-born baby who would grow up to marry Shelley and would write *Frankenstein*.

In *Snow White*, the picture of Snow White lying unconscious (after a visit from the wicked stepmother) was inspired by a photograph taken by the American photographer Lee Miller at the end of the war. The young girl is the daughter of a Nazi. He had shot himself, and the rest of the family were all poisoned. So you can imagine how much I enjoyed doing *The Emperor's New Clothes*. For once I was allowed to do something funny.

Once I've got the drawings and the composition more or less plotted out, I stick it to the window with masking tape (I haven't got a light-box) and then I trace it all off on to beautiful handmade watercolour paper. Then, having made any last-minute alterations, I draw the whole thing with great precision in pencil. At that stage, in black and white, it looks just like a page from a colouring book. Then I set to work with a mixture of watercolour, gouache and coloured pencils.

Angela Barrett: from *Snow White* by Josephine Poole, 1991

Angela Barrett: from *Snow White* by Josephine Poole, 1991

following pages Angela Barrett: from *Candide or Optimism* by Voltaire, 1996

..... each shot three bullets into his skull in the most peaceful way in the world,

23.

Chapter III

Candide decided to find somewhere else to pursue his
reasoning into cause and effect.

Patrick Benson

Born 1956.
Studied in Florence;
and at Chelsea
School of Art and
St Martin's School
of Art, London.

Although I have tried my hand at writing my own text, most of my illustration has been for other people's books. I've been incredibly lucky with authors – people like William Mayne, Russell Hoban, Roald Dahl, Martin Wadell, Kathy Henderson and, of course, Kenneth Grahame.

I think the most important thing an illustrator has to do is to provide lots of visual clues, bits of information – rather like snapshots – that will act as a sort of springboard for the imagination and help the child to visualise the surroundings in which the story is happening. And yes, I do quite a lot of preparatory drawings.

The people who've inspired me and influenced the way I work are many and various. They range from Fritz Wegner, who was my tutor at St Martins, and is a wonderful illustrator, Edward Ardizzone, E.H. Shepard – he really was a genius, he drew so much better than any of us – Heath Robinson, Tunnicliffe, Cecil Aldin and right back to Hokusai and Dürer. As a child I was entranced by some books my grandmother gave me. They came from Paris at the turn of the century – huge books about Napoleon, Frederick the Great and the Sun King, with illustrations by Job and Maurice Lenoir. I think we all borrow a little here and there, even if we don't let on.

It can be difficult deciding on a text, but I've had a lot of help from good editors – *Owl Babies*, for example, was something I might well have overlooked. I mean, if you just read the words, what have you got? The answer is, three baby owls, their mum flies off, the babies get worried and the mum comes back. Quite honestly, I didn't get it. But my editor rightly identified it as a perfect picture-book text, talked me into it, and it's my most successful book. It was complicated to do, though. Usually I start with a pen and ink drawing on which I apply the colour. In the case of *Owl Babies*, because it's a night-time story, I wanted it very dark, but I also wanted rich colours. I solved it by transferrring the black and white drawing on to clear film, then, lifting the film, I coloured underneath.

One thing I'm always conscious of is that illustrations can fail. I'm well aware of the dangers. I know that the wrong illustrations can literally destroy a dream and, however powerful the text, it's the images that stick in the mind.

from *The Lord Fish* by Walter de la Mare, 1997   opposite and next double page from *The MinPins* by Roald Dahl, 1991

Patrick Benson: from *The Sea-Thing Child* by Russell Hoban, 1999

Stephen Biesty

Born 1961.
Studied at
Brighton Polytechnic
and City of
Birmingham
Polytechnic.

I got into this because of an interest in history – visual history. As a child I spent a lot of time drawing cathedrals and castles. I suppose, deep down, it stems from a sort of curiosity really. I always liked looking at buildings, working out how they were made. When you start to draw a building, for example, as you get to grips with the perspective, you begin to understand how it works, how it's put together, and with cutaways you can explore it even further. And you can look at a place and uncover the layers of history that have accumulated over the years.

I always put figures in. As an illustrator you quickly catch on to the fact that nobody's going to look at it if there's no human interest. Figure drawing I can cope with as long as the figures are no bigger than about five centimetres. When you start including figures, you can begin to create a sense of atmosphere, you can show how the people related to the space, and you can explore the realities, the practicalities of the place, how people lived, how they adapted to their surroundings, how they slept, how they ate. There's really no end to the amount of detail you can include. I've always enjoyed looking at paintings by Brueghel and Bosch, and films like *El Cid*. They offer an enormous amount of period detail. Other influences would be the work of the illustrator David Macaulay, and Alan Sorrell, who did so much in the field of historical reconstruction.

There's a huge amount of research, the work itself is very laborious, and so it all takes a long time – often as long as fifteen months to complete one book.

I always work same size. I draw with a pencil initially, and then I work on top of that with ink, usually a Rotring needle-point pen, but sometimes I prefer to draw with a fine brush which gives the line a little variety, a little texture. Then of course I add colour and atmosphere with watercolour washes. I don't use a computer and I don't think I ever will.

I work such a long day on these books so I don't do much drawing for its own sake, though I do quite a lot of drawing with my son. He's very keen on steam engines so we go to steam rallies and take photographs, then come home and draw them.

opposite from *Incredible Explosions* by Richard Platt, 1996

following double page from *Man-of-War* by Richard Platt, 1993

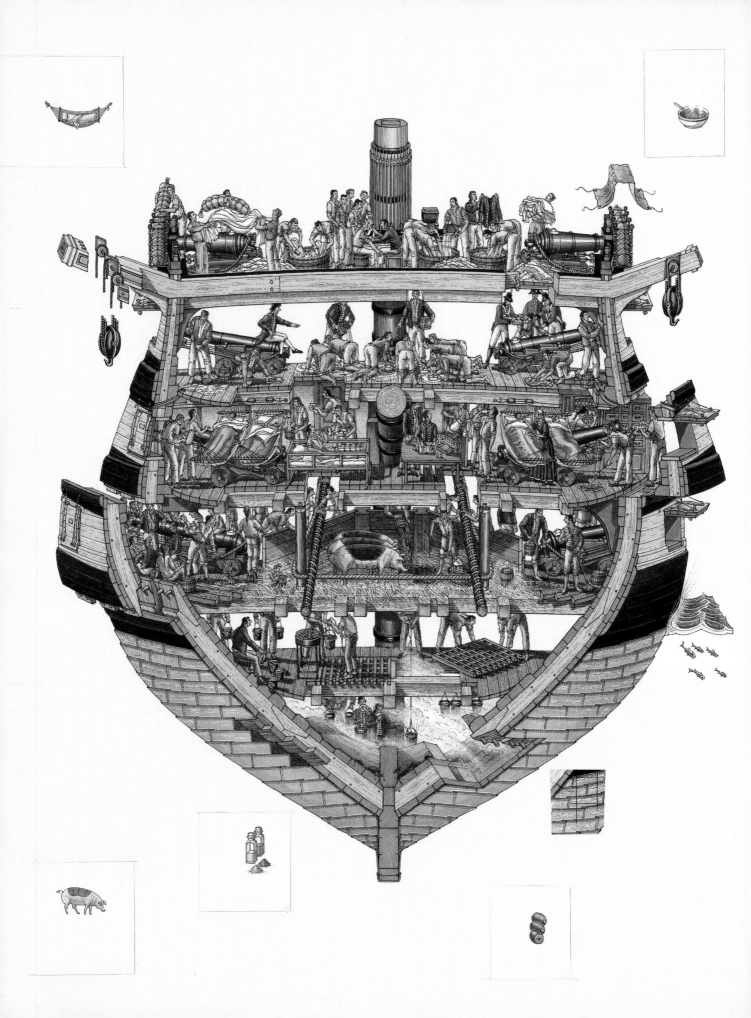

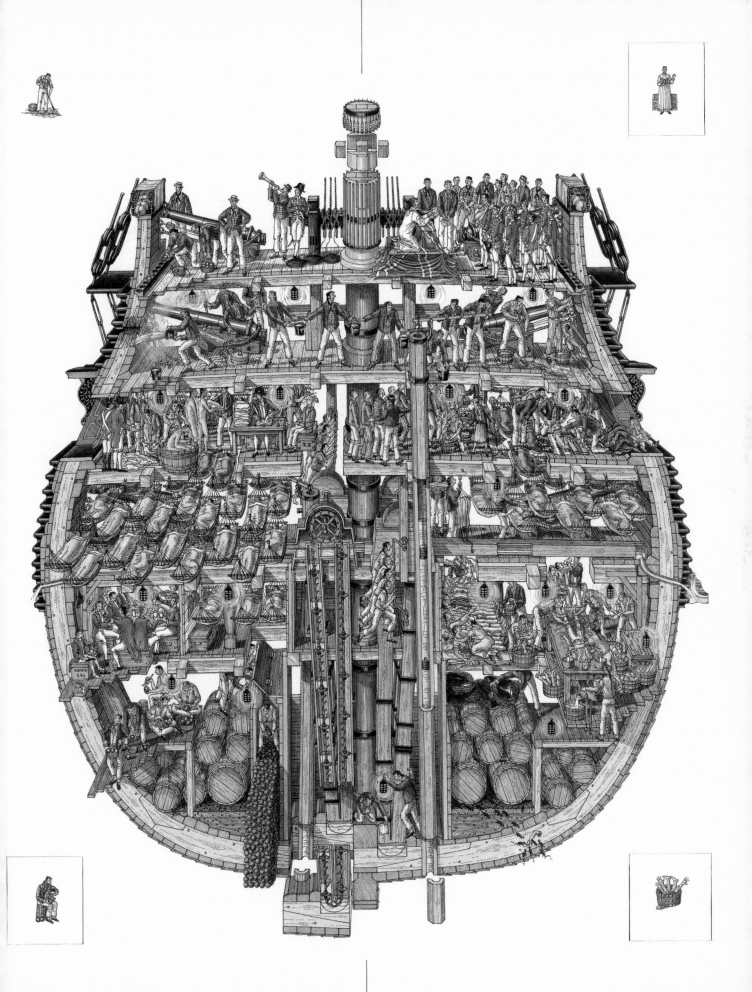

Stephen Biesty: from *Incredible Cross-Sections* by Richard Platt, 1992

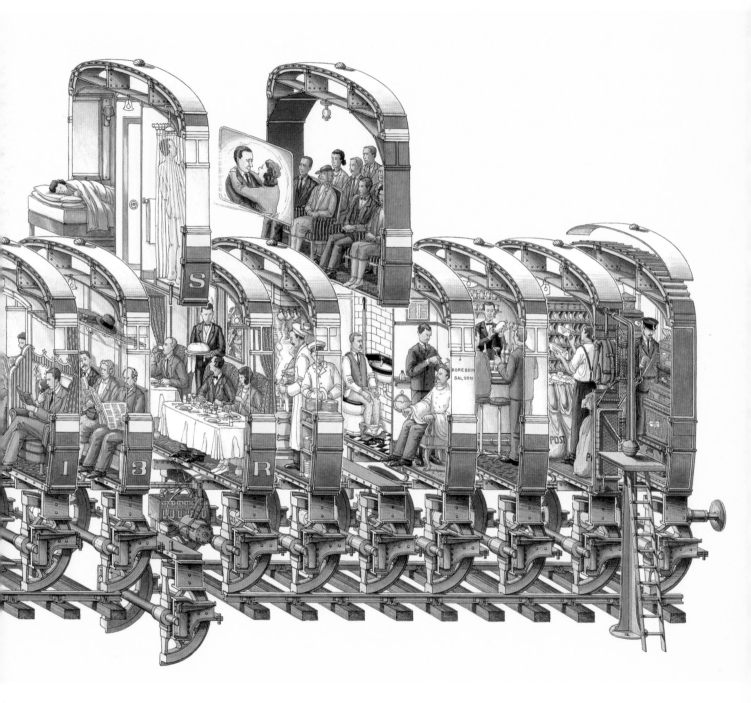

Quentin Blake

Born 1932.
Studied at
Downing College,
Cambridge;
the University of
London and
Chelsea School
of Art.

I started off doing cartoons for *Punch* when I was still at school. I went on to read English at Cambridge and then Education at London University and I didn't really get any art training until after I had stopped being a student. The drawings for *Punch* and *The Spectator* gave me something to live on, and I became a part-time student at Chelsea Art School for a couple of years. I used to go to life-classes two days a week, because up to then I just didn't know enough about how bodies worked to allow my drawings to develop. I also got the benefit of the advice and support of Brian Robb; knowing him really changed my life because, not long after, he moved to the Royal College of Art and eventually gave me a part-time job teaching there and I was there for twenty years. It really was the structure of my life.

It was while I was doing the magazine drawings that I came upon the possibilities of spontaneity – that you didn't have to be frightened. That kind of drawing is the basic act that for me makes illustration so attractive, though when I got into books I discovered that there were a lot of other aspects that also sustained my interest – trying to imagine the characters and the way they move and the kind of expressions they make, and then getting the right way of drawing for the particular book, and disposing the pictures properly so that they can help each other and make a sequence.

In a way I think my university time has stood me in quite good stead. I get a lot of pleasure and stimulus from reading and illustrating other people's writing, and what I learned about teaching helped to tell me something about how books work. A picture book has an effect on the reader not so very different from a good lesson.

I like organising a book, which means that I often have to reconcile spontaneous drawing with quite a high level of planning. When I was doing Sylvia Plath's *The Bed Book*, it must have been around 1970, I started using a light-box. It seemed like some kind of sin at the time, but it was enormously helpful, and since then I use one constantly. I put a sheet of watercolour paper over a rough and then, because I can see where everything has to go, I can draw as if I was making it up for the first time – actually feeling the gestures and expressions with the pen. I think that's why I don't get bored with it – that and the fact that you never know what you are going to read or think

from *The BFG* by Roald Dahl, 1982

opposite *Quentin Blake's ABC*, 1989

Quentin Blake: *Ten Frogs*, 1998

following double page Quentin Blake: *The Green Ship*, 1998

Raymond Briggs

Born 1934.
Studied at
Wimbledon School
of Art and the
Slade School of
Fine Art, London.

I didn't read much as a child and during the war I didn't have comics because of the paper shortage; but after the war I used to see the odd *Beano* or *Dandy,* and in those days the *Daily Mirror* had a whole page of comic strips. I chose the comic strip form for the *Father Christmas* books simply because picture books have a fixed number of pages – usually 32 – and that wasn't nearly enough for everything I wanted to put in, and a comic strip seemed a good solution. So I bought lots of comics and studied the form.

I was helped with *Father Christmas* by the fact that my dad was a milkman, so I knew something about the working conditions of people who have to deliver things, and I could imagine what a hell of a job that was – freezing cold, lonely, unsociable hours – enough to make anyone a bit grumpy.

I don't think about age groups – people can decide for themselves what they read. And I don't really plan ahead – usually stories just happen, except *The Snowman,* which was a very conscious reaction to *Fungus the Bogeyman* – after all that slime I really felt the need for something clean and pleasant.

I always used to draw in pencil, then go over it with ink, but then one day some friends asked me why it was I did really nice sensitive pencil drawings and then mucked them all up with ink. And it was true, they *were* losing a lot of their freshness. Have you ever seen rough drawings by any of the Victorian illustrators? Their drawings are so full of life before they've been transferred to a woodblock and engraved by people like the Dalziel brothers. The engravings are wonderful, but very different in character from the original drawings. Anyway, to keep the spontaneity I now make photocopies of my pencil drawings, then work on those with colour. I make several copies, so the great thing is, if I muck it up I just start again, and I've still got the original drawing. And using crayons, I find the colour grows into the picture, and you get a certain softness.

I don't go out sketching. I often include landscapes in my books, but they just come out of my head. I don't draw from life at all – well that's not quite true, there are the odd occasions, and one in particular sticks in my mind: I was waiting for someone in a hospital, waiting for so long I got really bored, so I started watching people. People are so extraordinary. There was this tiny little woman at reception, really *exceptionally* small, and suddenly, looming over her at the desk, there was this enormous man who, even though he must have been about six foot seven, with vast shoulders, had somehow managed to find a jacket that was actually too big for him. Well, that's the sort of thing that can make me want to draw on the spot.

Raymond Briggs: *Ethel & Ernest*, 1998

following double page Raymond Briggs: *When the Wind Blows*, 1982

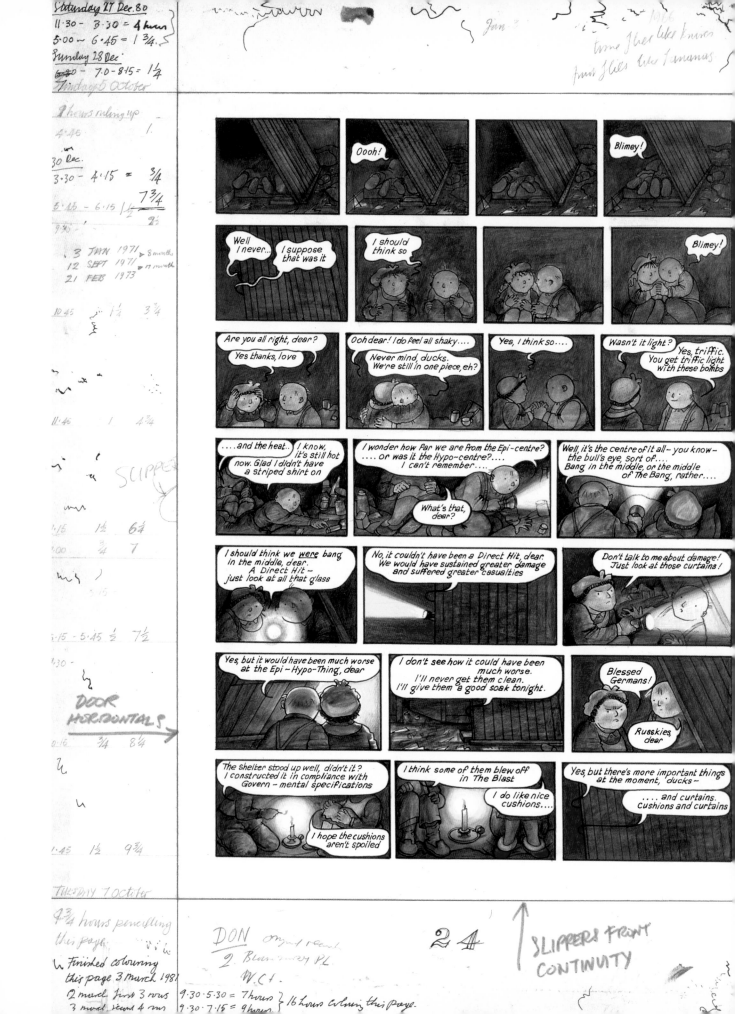

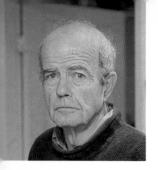

John Burningham

Born 1936.
Studied at Central
School of Art and
Design, London.

I don't think my attitude to my readers has changed over the years. I suppose that once I've had an idea for a book, the fact that it's for children is beside the point. Once I've got the idea, and I've begun to work on it, then I feel that above all my audience is not just children, it's much broader than that, it's people. And whilst I'm working towards simplification, I'm trying to steer away from childish things.

I try to draw as little as possible, keep it down to a bare minimum, just what's necessary; but I do masses of preparatory drawing. You have to. Drawing is like playing the piano, it's not a mechanical skill like bricklaying, and you have to practise constantly to keep it fluent.

The line is important, I suppose. When I draw I'm conscious of looking for a lively line – though what defines a lively line is difficult to say – but a bald outline would not be very interesting, obviously. A dipping pen is good – the weight of the line alters with the amount of pressure you put on it, so you get a bit of variety.

As for materials, I use a bit of everything, always have – ink, crayon, gouache, acrylic, photographs, cut paper, anything. I don't have rules, it just happens, and constantly takes me by surprise. I use a computer for cover designs, and for backgrounds – though not for *Cloudlands* – I took all those photographs myself. It took ages waiting for the right moment – waiting for sunsets, waiting for the rainbow which I finally got on the west coast of Ireland. People say I'm crazy and I could have done it on the computer but, I don't know, I've nothing against the computer, but it gives the work a different look somehow.

I never set myself boundaries, I don't have rules. It's a bit of a tightrope sometimes. With each new book I'll be thinking, can I do it again? Can I pull it off again? There are moments when I feel I've lost it, and that I have no ability. It only takes one slip and the whole thing wobbles and, well, that's a terrible moment. But then it all gets back on course. Even after forty years, it doesn't get any easier.

Aldo, 1991

opposite *Cloudland*, 1996

following double page *Whadayamean*, 1996

John Burningham: *Aldo*, 1991

Emma Chichester Clark

Born 1955.
Studied at Chelsea
School of Art and
the Royal College
of Art, London.

I think books for children should be wild and adventurous. They should offer you something you can escape into, something you don't get later on – it might be the only chance. It's the only time that children can develop their imagination, and it's so porous it's vital to fill it with extraordinary things, not mundane, boring things.

I started drawing just about as soon as I could hold a pencil. I drew all the time. But I could never find enough paper, and my mother wouldn't let me use her Basildon Bond. Then I noticed one day that grown-up books (hardbacks) always had a blank page at the beginning and the end, so I used to tear those out secretly and draw on them and make my own little books. I knew I was going to go on drawing all my life, and I took it for granted that that would be how I would earn a living. I loved the Madeleine books as a child and Babar, and Charles Addams.

Things were quite difficult when I was at Chelsea School of Art. We were all affected by the political tensions of that period. There was no illustration course at that time, just graphic design, and we used to do illustrations secretly and keep them hidden in our type specimen books. It was very frustrating. The teacher who fought hardest for drawing was the illustrator, Susan Einzig. She inspired us with her talk of Bonnard and Matisse and her enthusiasm for life drawing. And Linda Kitson generated a lot of enthusiasm and made us really want to draw. She addressed us as individuals, and communicated her own sense of excitement about the very act of drawing. After Chelsea, at the Royal College of Art, my tutor was Quentin Blake, whose pen and ink drawings I remembered so well from a book I'd enjoyed as a teenager.

I still draw with a pencil, just an ordinary pencil. I can't cope with pen and ink. And for colour, I'm completely addicted to Dr Martin's Radiant Concentrated Color. It's American, comes in little bottles, and it's much easier to use than ordinary watercolour. You can put layers and layers of colour, one on top of another.

from *Enchantment: Fairy Tales, Ghost Stories and Tales of Wonder*
selected by Kevin Crossley-Holland, 2000

opposite *It was You, Blue Kangaroo!*, 2000
following double page *No more Kissing!*, 2001

Emma Chichester Clark: from *Enchantment: Fairy Tales, Ghost Stories and Tales of Wonder*
selected by Kevin Crossley-Holland, 2000

Lauren Child

Born 1967.
Studied at
Manchester
Polytechnic and
City and Guilds
of London Art
School.

I always loved to draw. My father, who was an art teacher, was a great inspiration.
I did my sixth form at the school where he taught. He ran an amazing art department.
He really made you want to draw, made you look, made you understand things, whether
it was through drawing in a straightforward classical way, or learning about Cubism,
or Matisse or whatever.

Art school was a disappointment. Until I went there I never understood how
people could have thought life drawing was boring! There was no sense of discovery
or excitement about it there, so I left after a year. I did a course in decorative arts at
an independent art school and eventually found my way back to my original intention,
which was to create books for children.

Books I particularly remember from my childhood are the Madeline books by
Bemelmans – they have such mood and atmosphere. And I liked the expressive quality
of Quentin Blake's scribbly images. I loved E.H. Shepard, and Carl Larssen, but my
greatest source of inspiration has been Snoopy and the boldness and simplicity of those
drawings. They appeal across the generations.

I use a computer for a lot of the work. I use it more and more as I get better at it.
I put together backgrounds made up of all sorts of elements – photographs, collages,
etc. After that I can superimpose the figures.

I draw the figures in pencil rather than ink. I just can't use pen and ink. I know it's
meant to be the most spontaneous medium, but people using pen and ink usually draw
over a pencil line, don't they? So I just use pencil, it's much less inhibiting and I can rub
it out if it goes wrong. Then I scan the pencil drawing into the computer, clean up the
line, and print it in black on cartridge paper so I can then continue to work on it with
paints, collage or whatever. Then I cut the figures out and scan them into the computer
again. I love the computer, because it's so flexible, it keeps the whole thing fluid – and
I can juggle things round until I'm happy with the look of it – sometimes a drawing might
be just right, but the scale might be wrong, in which case I can keep the spontaneity
of the drawing by re-sizing it, rather than having to draw it all over again.

And I say,

"Are you sure?

Really?

One

of these?"

Lauren Child: *I Will not Ever Never Eat a Tomato*, 2000

When we get home we find Grandad is missing.
Uncle Ted phones round all the neighbours
and is about to dial 999 when
Mrs Stampney at Number 9
calls to say she has found Grandad
sitting
in
her
sitting room.

Watching the racing.

She's quite grumpy about it.

Lauren Child: *My Uncle is a Hunkle says Clarice Bean*, 2000

Uncle Ted says,

How in tarnation did you end up here?

Grandad says,
        All the houses look the same,
    it's a job to tell them apart without my glasses.

    But I know it's really because
    Mrs Stampney's got a bigger television set than us
            and it's got a remote control.

My sister Marcie has a room of her own,
so she has peace and quiet whenever she fancies.
Marcie likes to wear make-up and read about boys.
When I have time on my hands I peep
round the door and try to make her
notice me.

She says,

Go away.

And I say,

Why?

**Because
I don't want to talk to you.**

Why?

**Because
you are very irritating.**

Why?

**Because
you are a little brat.**

Why?

**You better get
out of my room
before I count to ten.**

And I don't need to ask why.

do boys
give you the
dreamy eye?

???

Maarcie

Lauren Child: *Clarice Bean, That's Me!*, 1999

Sara Fanelli

Born 1969.
Studied at
City and Guilds of
London Art School,
Camberwell
School of Art and
the Royal College of
Art, London.

As a child, I was always drawing, always making little books. I knew I wanted to be an illustrator. With a mother who was an art historian and a father who taught history of architecture, I grew up surrounded by unusual books, and I was intrigued by the work of Mayakovsky, Lissitzky, Kurt Schwitters, and the Bauhaus.

I came to London to study because I felt that art schools here would allow me to focus on a personal, experimental approach, which I don't think would have been possible at home in Italy.

I developed an interest in collage in an attempt to move away from the flat colours I'd been using in my painting on the BA course, and because of the vast number of bits and pieces I'd collected. When I make a collage illustration, I start with a drawing of the composition, the layout. Then I play around with it, interweaving the narrative with all the different items I might be using – a piece of paper, say; maybe a piece that already comes with a story of its own, with curious stains or marks on it, a sweet wrapper, perhaps; a piece of my grandmother's writing – a shopping list, for example. Handwriting in an unexpected context is very evocative. All sorts of references and ephemera, things that hopefully will invite you back for a second or third reading. I like to play around with the typography too, and create my own lettering. Too many designers rely on computers for that.

I do a lot of drawing from reality. I like to take myself away to another city, like Barcelona, for example, where I explore the place, visiting the museums, keeping a sketch book, then I'll put aside all these ideas until I need them.

I also enjoy printmaking, etching in particular, and sometimes I'll cut up the prints and use them in my collages. I don't use a computer to create artwork. Some people have assumed that there are images in *It's Dreamtime* which are computer generated, but they aren't – they are photograms. I create the different textures by sprinkling the surface with things like sugar, lentils, and spaghetti. Oh, and rice. Rice is very good at that.

opposite *Dear Diary*, 2000

PEGASUS

Sara Fanelli: *Mythological Creatures*, 2002

Sara Fanelli: *Dog's Life*, 1998

Michael Foreman

Born 1932.
Studied at
Lowestoft Art School;
St Martin's School
of Art, London
and the Royal College
of Art, London.

I was obsessed with drawing as a child, but I never dreamt it could actually be a 'job'.
I attended a free Saturday art class at Lowestoft art college. At 15, I left school to study
painting full time, after which I came to London, to St Martin's. Then I went to the Royal
College of Art, where I studied graphics. Illustration as such wasn't taught in those
days. Ardizzone was one of my teachers. I think I was very lucky to have started
art school so young, and luckier still that art schools in those (pre-formaldehyde,
pre-conceptual) days actually taught Art. It was a rigorous training, not just painting
and drawing from life, but hours of anatomy and perspective – boring at the time,
but it really taught you to understand what you were looking at. But art schools
have changed now. I've done a bit of teaching but I gave it up. I felt uneasy teaching
illustration to people who hadn't yet learnt to draw.

As a student I did a lot of freelance work, learning to respond instantly to text by
drawing for newspapers and even, at one point, working for the police, drawing female
suspects in the days when Identikit only catered for men. I was lucky enough to get a
travel scholarship which took me all round the world, working as a 'commercial artist'
on all sorts of projects, drawing landscapes, architecture, wildlife, everything. That was
an education in itself.

I used to read all the comics, because my mum ran the village shop and I delivered
the newspapers, but I grew up completely without books. All we had at home was the
family bible, so I never read any fairy tales or classics until I was an adult. But I think this
was an advantage when I started as a book illustrator. I was able to approach all the
old classics without being influenced by anyone else's interpretation. Though when I'm
working on books with a historical background I would admit to being influenced by
the work of certain painters, like Brueghel and Bosch: it's all the period detail they give
you, especially in crowd scenes.

I can't say the work gets any easier. In many ways I keep making it more difficult for
myself, trying to make things more real, not in a literal, photographic sense, but in an
emotional sense, telling a story by capturing the essence of the situation, giving it some
meaning. Ardizzone did it, not just in books, but also as a war artist, and Quentin Blake
does it. It's a question of creating another world, believable in its own right. It's all in
the drawing.

opposite from *Seasons of Splendour: Tales, Myths and Legends of India* by Madhur Jaffrey, 1985

following double page *War Game*, 1993

The bombing of Pakefield Church 1941

Michael Foreman: *War Boy: A Country Childhood*, 1989

Tony Ross

Born 1938.
Studied at
Liverpool School
of Art.

One of the first things I realised when I was studying illustration at art school was that most illustrators, with a few exceptions, like Tomi Ungerer, or Saul Steinberg, only work in one style, which they stick to for the rest of their life. And I realised early on that I didn't want to commit myself in that way. My work changes according to the text. It's such a great luxury to read a text and just draw, without worrying about 'style'. And it's good to keep changing – it makes you feel you're still learning something.

Having worked as a teacher of illustration, obviously I have had to talk about style; also the fact that in order to develop a way of working you have to learn certain rules, and only when you know and understand the rules can you throw them away.

Line is the most important element in my work. I trained as an etcher, where you are dealing with a black line, and for me the line is the basis of the whole thing. If it works in line, it works. If it doesn't work in line, it's no good. To me, colour always comes second.

I draw mostly with what I call a post-office pen – a dip pen. It all depends on the nib. I had one nib for about twenty years. It was perfect, all scratchy, bendy, blunt, and full of character. When it finally broke I had a terrible job replacing it. I bought hundreds of nibs but I couldn't get on with them. Like a lot of new boys, they seemed to have no personality to begin with.

As well as illustrating lots of contemporary authors, I've done quite a lot of re-illustration – *Just William*, *Pippi Longstocking*, *The Picture of Dorian Gray*, *Worzel Gummidge* and *Alice in Wonderland* and *Through the Looking-Glass*. Having Tenniel looking over my shoulder wasn't too much of a problem, because although I like them now, as a child I didn't enjoy his illustrations. So I didn't feel inhibited by any sense of paying homage to him. But I could never do *Winnie the Pooh*. Those are the greatest children's books ever. Head and shoulders above everything else. Shepard's drawing has such visual charm, and he knew how to put the text first, and it all meshes together so perfectly.

Tony Ross: *I Want My Potty*, 1986

I want to break in broncos
and twirl my rope lasso

Tony Ross: from *I Want to be a Cowgirl* by Jeanne Willis, 2001

I've got my shiny spurs and boots
I've got my cowgirl hat

Susan Swings

Tony Ross: from *Susan Laughs* by Jeanne Willis, 1999

That is Susan
Through and through
Just like me
Just like you

Posy Simmonds

Born 1945.
Studied at Central
School of Art and
Design, London.

I grew up in the shadow of an enormous bookcase full of bound copies of *Punch* dating
from the 1900s and 1930s. There were also *Giles* annuals and collections of drawings
by Pont and Ronald Searle, which I used to pore over. So my childhood drawings always
had captions and conversations and have done ever since, really. I love the combination
of words and pictures, the way they can complement or illuminate or contradict
each other.

I studied fine art briefly, then swapped to graphic design, a mainly typographic course
but useful for learning hand lettering. After art school I began drawing for newspapers –
very occasional and tiny space fillers to begin with, and after a year or two, more regular
cartoons and illustrations in various things. Before I did a weekly strip in *The Guardian*
I was a sort of dogsbody on their features pages, doing drawings to fill in holes for all
kinds of articles. They'd ring and say, 'There's a hole this big, can you fill it by five o'clock?'
Sometimes the space was weeny, sometimes across six columns. The time pressure
meant drawing quickly, no time for second thoughts, using a hefty line because in those
days the reproduction was terrible. I used a felt tip pen or a broad nib Rotring. In recent
years the reproduction has got much better. For *Gemma Bovery* I was able to use a finer
pen, crayon, and tone with grey wash.

I usually draw with my right hand, though I am ambidextrous. My style is looser with
my left hand. It's the hand that does practical things, like cutting out, and sharpening
pencils. Drawing for newspapers was usually in black and white. Doing a children's book
was my first chance to use colour. I found this difficult – there are so many colours, too
much choice. I didn't find it hard to move from writing for adults to writing for children.

I do a lot of drawing, masses of doodling, but I don't go out drawing in the street
because people always want to see what you're doing. Instead I just go round looking
at people. I'm incredibly nosy – so I take a good look at anything that catches my eye –
someone's shoes, say, or eyebrows. Then I go home and get it down on paper.

opposite *Gemma Bovery*, 1999
following double page studies from sketchbook for *Gemma Bovery*, 1999

large lumpen peasants

french lessons
conversation.

Roxana

hair put up
with scrunchie

bright red
nose

shaved
armpits

70 kilos

uneven
sunburn

cellulite

badly
shaved
legs

mosquito
bites

smells
of jungle
juice
& sun cream

English shorts

French legs

heavy &
earthenware
terra cotta
enamel plates etc

bought in the 80's
in Habitat, now
chipped & stained

Italo/Med cuisine
polenta tomatoes
pasta basil - couscous
cheap local wine from Co-op
(disgusting) bought by
the litre
in plastic
jerry cans

one spoon fork
knife & plate
for the whole
meal

kitchen paper
round the neck
plate mopped
with bread

breath
always smelt strongly of garlic

dobs of butter

brioches

Gemma came to hate those
Sunday lunches.... HATED the relish
which greeted every dish... hated the
the finger-licking, the mopping-up with
bread, the patted stomachs...the
swallowed belches.... HATED the
moment when Charlie finally would
wiped his chin with kitchen paper,
raised another tumbler of disgusting
wine and sighed:
    "Haaaaa – THIS is the Life! eh!
Cheery-weeries, all!

Posy Simmonds: *Fred,* 1987

Charlotte Voake

Born 1957.
Studied at
the University
of London.

I always drew from an early age but I didn't go to art school, partly because my parents didn't want me to, and partly, I think, because of a lack of confidence. I did go to a few art classes but found myself terribly worried by how good everyone else was at it. It was a dreadful worry. I felt that in an art school I would have been too inhibited to get anything done at all. Instead I did a degree in art history. But I always wanted to be an illustrator. I remember, when I was about five, a friend of the family came to our house and he was an illustrator. I don't know who he was, but he made a great impression on me when he said, 'What shall I draw for you? I'll draw anything you like.' I suppose I just loved the idea of being able to draw anything and everything. It was a real inspiration.

I don't use any pencil under-drawing, I just draw with ink, over and over again – doodle, doodle, doodle – until suddenly it's right and I think, 'Aha! That's how it should be.' So it gets all higgledy-piggledy over the page. It evolves as I go along. But I am becoming more interested in discipline.

If there's something in the story that I am going to have to draw again and again – like the child skipping in *Elsie Piddock* – then I'll prepare for that by drawing it from life so often that it becomes second nature. Fortunately my son, William, who was about the right age, would skip for hours on end while I drew him.

I've always found the work of Ardizzone to be a great source of inspiration, and I've also been very influenced by the drawings and engravings of certain 18th-century artists. I love the way they developed a sort of graphic shorthand, especially when they drew trees. And the way I do eyes, with little dots, it's something I got from reading about the sculptor Bernini. Apparently when he was carving a portrait bust he found that the tiny dots he put on the marble to represent the position of the eyes immediately gave the whole thing its character – so I tried it on paper and it works very well – so that's a sort of shorthand too. And it's a very useful solution, because I find that if you draw the eyes in great detail the whole thing becomes stiff, too fixed. There's no room for imagination on the part of the person who's looking at it.

this page, opposite and following double page from *The Best of Aesop's Fables* retold by Margaret Clark, 1990

final double page *Alphabet Adventure*, 1999

Cc castle

Dd dragon

Selected list of published books

Books illustrated by the artists in chronological sequence

Angela Barrett

The King, the Cat and the Fiddle by Yehudi Menuhin
    and Christopher Hope
The Walker Book of Ghost Stories compiled by
    Susan Hill
Through the Kitchen Window by Susan Hill
Through the Garden Gate by Susan Hill
Can it be true? by Susan Hill
Snow White by Josephine Poole
The Hidden House by Martin Waddell
Beware, Beware by Susan Hill
Candide or Optimism by Voltaire
The Emperor's New Clothes by Hans Christian
    Andersen, translated by Naomi Lewis
Joan of Arc by Josephine Poole
Orchard Book of Stories from the Ballet by
    Geraldine McCaughrean
Rocking Horse Land compiled by Naomi Lewis
The Orchard Book of Shakespeare Stories
    retold by Andrew Matthews

Patrick Benson

The Hob Stories by William Mayne
The Tough Princess by Martin Waddell
Herbert: Five Stories by Ivor Cutler
The Baron all at Sea adapted by Adrian Mitchell
Fred the Angel by Martin Waddell
Robin Hood by Sarah Hayes
Little Penguin
Fly Fishing by J.R. Hartley
The MinPins by Roald Dahl
Toad Triumphant by William Horwood
Owl Babies by Martin Waddell
The Little Boat by Kathy Henderson
The Willows and Beyond by William Horwood
The Lord Fish by Walter de la Mare
Let the Lynx Come In by Jonathan London
The Six Swan Brothers by Adele Geras
The Sea-Thing Child by Russell Hoban
Squeak's Good Idea by Max Eilenberg
Mole and the Baby Bird

Stephen Biesty

Explore the World of Man-made Wonders
    by Simon Adams
Exploring the Past: Ancient Egypt by George Hare
Incredible Cross-Sections by Richard Platt
Man-of-War by Richard Platt
Castle by Richard Platt
Incredible Explosions by Richard Platt
Incredible Body by Richard Platt
Gold: A Treasure Hunt through Time
    by Meredith Hooper

Quentin Blake

Patrick
Jack and Nancy
Angelo
Snuff
*How Tom beat Captain Najork and his
    Hired Sportsmen* by Russell Hoban
Danny Champion of the World by Roald Dahl
The Adventures of Lester
The Enormous Crocodile by Roald Dahl
Custard and Company by Ogden Nash
Mr Magnolia
The Twits by Roald Dahl
George's Marvellous Medicine by Roald Dahl
Revolting Rhymes by Roald Dahl
The BFG by Roald Dahl
Quentin Blake's Nursery Rhyme Book
The Witches by Roald Dahl
The Story of the Dancing Frog
Dirty Beasts by Roald Dahl
The Giraffe, the Pelly and Me by Roald Dahl
Mrs Armitage on Wheels
Matilda by Roald Dahl
Rhyme Stew by Roald Dahl
All Join In
Esio Trot by Roald Dahl
Dahl Diary by Roald Dahl
Algernon and other Cautionary Tales
    by Hilaire Belloc
Simpkin
Cockatoos
The Quentin Blake Book of Nonsense Verse
My Year by Roald Dahl
Featherbrains by John Yeoman
The Singing Tortoise by John Yeoman
Family Album by John Yeoman
Roald Dahl's Revolting Recipes by Roald Dahl
The Do-It-Yourself House that Jack Built
    by John Yeoman
Mr Nodd's Ark by John Yeoman
The Winter Sleepwalker by Joan Aiken
Charlie and the Chocolate Factory by Roald Dahl
Charlie and the Great Glass Elevator by Roald Dahl
James and the Giant Peach by Roald Dahl
The Magic Finger by Roald Dahl
Clown
The Quentin Blake Book of Nonsense Stories
Fantastic Mr Fox by Roald Dahl
The Princes' Gifts by John Yeoman
Up with Birds! by John Yeoman
The Green Ship
Quentin Blake's ABC
Mrs Armitage and the Big Wave
Fantastic Daisy Artichoke
Ten Frogs
The Heron and the Crane by John Yeoman
The Laureate's Party
Because a Fire was in my Head
    edited by Michael Morpurgo

Raymond Briggs

The Strange House
Midnight Adventure
Ring-A-Ring O'Roses
Fee Fi Fo Fum
The Mother Goose Treasury
The Fairy Tale Treasury
Father Christmas
Father Christmas Goes on Holiday
Fungus the Bogeyman
The Snowman
The Tin-Pot Foreign General and the Old Iron Woman
When the Wind Blows
Unlucky Wally Twenty Years On
The Man
The Bear
Ethel & Ernest
Ug: Boy Genius of the Stone Age

John Burningham

John Burningham's ABC
Trubloff
Chitty, Chitty, Bang, Bang by Ian Fleming
Humbert
Cannonball Simp
Harquin
The Extra-ordinary Tug-of-War
Seasons
Mr Gumpy's Outing
Around the World in Eighty Days
Mr Gumpy's Motor Car
Little Books series: *The Baby, The Rabbit, The
    School, The Snow*
Little Book series: *The Blanket, The Cupboard,
    The Dog, The Friend*
The Adventures of Humbert, Simp and Harquin
Come Away from the Water, Shirley
Time to Get Out of the Bath, Shirley
Would You Rather
The Shopping Basket
Avocado Baby
John Burningham's Number Play Series
The Window in the Willows by Kenneth Grahame
Granpa
Play and Learn Books: *ABC, 123, Opposites, Colours*
Where's Julius?
*John Patrick Norman McHennessy – The Boy
    who is Always Late*
Oi! Get Off Our Train
Aldo
England
Harvey Slumfenburger's Christmas Present
Courtney
Cloudland
France
Whadayamean
Getting On with Getting On

Emma Chichester Clark

Catch that Hat!
The Story of Horrible Hilda and Henry
Stuff and Nonsense edited by Laura Cecil
Cissy Lavender
Wild Robert by Diana Wynne Jones
Boo! Stories to Make You Jump by Laura Cecil
Ragged Robin by James Reeves
I Never Saw a Purple Cow
The Queen's Goat by Margaret Mahy
Orchard Book of Greek Myths
    by Geraldine McCaughrean
The Way of the Cat
The Minstrel and the Dragon Pup
    by Rosemary Sutcliff
Ruth and the Blue Horse by Charles Ashton
Goodnight Stella by Kate McMullan
James and the Giant Peach by Roald Dahl
Mrs Vole the Vet by Allan Ahlberg
More!
The Adventures of Robin Hood and Maid Marian
    edited by Adrian Mitchell
I Love You, Blue Kangaroo!
Sleeping Beauty by Adele Geras
Follow my Leader!
Swan Lake by Adele Geras
Mrs Bilberry's New House
It was You, Blue Kangaroo!
Enchantment: Fairy Tales, Ghost Stories
    and Tales of Wonder selected
    by Kevin Crossley-Holland
Elf Hill: Tales from Hans Christian Andersen
    selected by Naomi Lewis
No More Kissing!
Where are you, Blue Kangaroo?
Mimi's Book of Opposites

Lauren Child

Addy the Baddy by Margaret Joy
I want a Pet
Clarice Bean, That's Me!
I Will not Ever Never eat a Tomato
My Uncle is a Hunkle says Clarice Bean
My Dream Bed
I am not Sleepy and Will not go to Bed
What Planet are you From, Clarice Bean?
Definitely Daisy: You're a Disgrace by Jenny Oldfield
Definitely Daisy: I'd Like a Little Word, Leonie
    by Jenny Oldfield
Definitely Daisy: You Must be Joking, Jimmy
    by Jenny Oldfield
Definitely Daisy: Not now, Nathan! by Jenny Oldfield
Definitely Daisy: What's the matter, Maya?
    by Jenny Oldfield
Beware the Story Book Wolves
Dan's Angel by Alexander Sturgis
Definitely Daisy: Just you Wait, Winona
    by Jenny Oldfield
Utterly me, Clarice Bean

Sara Fanelli

Button
My Map Book
Wolf
Pinocchio: Picture Box
Cinderella: Picture Box
Dibby Dubby Dhu by George Baker
Dog's Life
It's Dreamtime
Dear Diary
Alphabicycle Order by Christopher Reid
The New Faber Book of Children's Verse,
    edited by Matthew Sweeney
First Flight
Mythological Creatures

Michael Foreman

The Perfect Present
The Two Giants
The Great Sleigh Robbery
Horatio
Moose
Dinosaurs and all that Rubbish
War and Peas
All The King's Horses
Panda and His Voyage of Discovery
Trick a Tracker
Panda and the Old Lion
Land of Dreams
Panda and the Bunyips
Cat and Canary
Panda and the Bushfire
Ben's Box
The Saga of Erik the Viking by Terry Jones
Ben's Baby
The Angel and the Wild Animal
War Boy: A Country Childhood
Oneworld
World of Fairytales
The Boy who sailed with Columbus
Jack's Fantastic Voyage
Grandfather's Pencil
War Game
Dad, I can't sleep
Surprise, surprise
After the War Was Over
Seal Surfer
The Little Reindeer
Look! Look!
Angel and the Box of Time
Land of the Long White Cloud
    by Kiri Te Kanawa
The Songs my Paddle Sings by James Riordan
Seasons of Splendour: Tales, Myths and
    Legends of India
    by Madhur Jaffrey
Jack's Big Race
Chicken Licken
Little Red Hen
Rock-a-Doodle Do
Saving Sinbad
Cat in the Manger
Wonder Goal!

Tony Ross

The Reluctant Vampire by Eric Morecambe
Vampire Park by Willis Hall
Towser series: *I'm coming to get you*
Limericks by Michael Palin
I Want My Potty
Oscar got the Blame
Super Dooper Jezebel
Fantastic Mr Fox by Roald Dahl
I Want a Cat
A Fairy Tale
Don't Do That
Through the Looking Glass
How to be a Little Sod by Simon Brett
Alice's Adventures in Wonderland (abridged)
Red Eyes at Night by Michael Morpurgo
Meet Just William by Richmal Compton
Susan Laughs by Jeanne Willis
I Want to be a Cowgirl by Jeanne Willis
Pippi Longstocking by Astrid Lindgren

Posy Simmonds

Bear Book
Mrs Weber's Diary
True Love
Pick of Posy
Bouncing Buffalo
Very Posy
Pure Posy
Fred
Lulu and the Flying Babies
The Chocolate Wedding
Matilda, who told such Dreadful Lies
    by Hilaire Belloc
Mustn't Grumble
F-Freezing ABC
Cautionary Tales by Hilaire Belloc
Gemma Bovery
Lavender

Charlotte Voake

The Way to the Sattin Shore by Philippa Pearce
The Ghost Child by Emma Tennant
Tom's Cat
Over The Moon
Bad Egg: The True Story of Humpty Dumpty
    by Sarah Hayes
Mrs Goose's Baby
First Things First
Duck by David Lloyd
Amy Said by Martin Waddell
The Best of Aesop's Fables retold by Margaret Clark
Three Little Pigs and Other Bedtime Stories
Caterpillar, Caterpillar by Vivian French
The Ridiculous Story of Gammer Gurton's Needle
    by David Lloyd
Mr Davies and the Baby
Fur by Jan Mark
Ginger
Alphabet Adventure
Here Comes the Train!
Elsie Piddock Skips in Her Sleep
Pizza Kittens

THE BRITISH LIBRARY

Acknowledgments

The organisers of *Magic Pencil* wish to thank the following for their help
in the production of the exhibition and book:
Nick Ardizzone, Avril Brodey, Karen Brookfield, Sue Corfield, Nick Hawker,
Richard Hill, Helen Hutton, Yasmin Kenyani, Amanda Little, Phil McBride, Tina Miller,
Nikki Mansergh, Fergus Muir, Michael Parkin, Sarah Packenham, Simon Shawcross,
Alex Tham, Books for Keeps, TV Cartoons Ltd, Illuminated Films Ltd,
Snowman Enterprises Ltd, King Rollo Films Ltd, 55degrees Ltd

The British Council:
Marcus Alexander, Dana Andrew, Katie Boot, Tony Connor, Jo Gutteridge,
Craig Henderson, Gareth Hughes, Mary Openshaw and Anna Simpson

The British Library:
Geraldine Kenny, Heather Norman-Soderlind, Alan Sterenberg
and David Way

Laing Art Gallery, Newcastle upon Tyne:
Julie Anderson, Samantha Hill and Julie Milne

Centre for the Children's Book, Newcastle upon Tyne:
Mary Briggs and Elizabeth Hammill

The organisers also wish to acknowledge the support of
Andersen Press, Random House and Walker Books
who have generously donated books for use during the exhibition

© The British Council and The British Library 2002
Catalogue texts © Quentin Blake, Joanna Carey and The British Council
Portraits of artists (details) © Toby Glanville

The publishers have made every effort to contact all copyright holders.
If proper acknowledgment has not been made, we ask all copyright holders
to contact the publishers.

Published by
The British Council, 10 Spring Gardens, London SW1A 2BN
and
The British Library, 96 Euston Road, St Pancras, London NW1 2DB

ISBN 0 7123 4770 4

Catalogue photography:
Rodney Todd-White & Son, London
The Ikon Partnership, Stockport, Cheshire
Bridgeman Art Library

Exhibition designed by Cottrell + Vermeulen
Built by E. Abrahams and Company Limited
Catalogue designed by Richard Hollis and Marit Münzberg
Cover designed by Quentin Blake
Printed in England by Butler & Tanner, Frome